REFERENCES.

No		No	
1	Kings Arms	41	London Hotel & Posting Ho
2	George Inn	42	Swan
3	Old Crown & Sceptre	43	Phœnix
4	Black Horse	44	Taunton Courier Office
5	All Balls School Room	45	Coach & Horses
6	Canal Office	46	Victoria
7	Turk's Head	47	Race Horse
8	Brannans Coffee House	48	Shakspeare
	& Reading Rooms	49	Barley Mow
9	Ring of Bells	50	Waggon & Horses
10	Church of England School	51	do do
11	Octagon Chapel	52	Rising Sun
9	Oxford Inn	53	Seven Stars
12	Black Boy	54	British & Foreign School
13	3 Three Tuns	55	Bleathleys Waggon Office
14	National School	56	Royal Marine
15	Huishs Alms Houses	57	Crown & Tower
4	Post Office	58	Theatre
6	West of England &	59	Baptist Chapel
	South Wales District Bank	60	Brices Waggon Office
17	Tutons Gin Shops	61	Mechanics Institution
8	King W.m IV.	62	Boot
12	Whitmash's Waggon Office	63	King & Queen
19	Fleur de Lis	64	Paul S.t Indep.t Chapel
19	Half Moon	65	Original Infant School
20	Register Office	66	Bird in Hand
21	Spread Eagle	67	Unitarian Chapel
22	Bear	68	Savings Bank
23	Nags Head	69	Saracens Head
24	Bristol Inn	70	Crown
25	Castle Hotel & Posting House	71	George Hotel & Posting Ho
26	Cockrells Hotel & Posting Ho	72	Bell
27	Winchester Arms	73	Green Dragon
28	Four Alls	74	Crown & Mitre
29	Friends Meeting House	75	Pig Market
30	Public Hall	76	Mariners Arms
31	Angel	77	Full Moon
32	Stukeys Banking Co	78	Blue Boy
33	New Market House	79	Royal Oak
33	Old do do	80	New Angel
34	White Hart	81	Wesleyan Method Chapel
35	Black Moor Badcock	82	Catholic Chapel
36	Chapels Gin Shop	83	Eye Infirmary
37	County Guards Office	84	Compasses
38	Norths Gin Shop	85	Sugar Loaf
39	Little Angel	86	Wilton Inn

St James Parish Colour'd Drab
St Marys do do Yellow
Do St Mary Magdalene do do Green
Wilton do do do Blue
Bishops Hull do do Brown

Jeboult's Taunton 1983
has been published as a Limited
Edition of which this is

Number **397**

A complete list of the
original subscribers is printed
at the back of the book

JEBOULT'S
TAUNTON

FRONT COVER: Edward Jeboult, aged 54, 1883 and south side of Fore
Street, c1865.

FRONTISPIECE: St Mary Magdalene's Church from the south-east, c1865.

JEBOULT'S
TAUNTON

A VICTORIAN RETROSPECT

BY

ROBIN BUSH

To ... with best wishes,
Robin Bush.

BARRACUDA BOOKS LIMITED
BUCKINGHAM, ENGLAND
MCMLXXXIII

PUBLISHED BY BARRACUDA BOOKS LIMITED
BUCKINGHAM, ENGLAND
AND PRINTED BY
HOLYWELL PRESS LIMITED
OXFORD, ENGLAND

BOUND BY
J W BRAITHWAITE & SON LIMITED
WOLVERHAMPTON, ENGLAND

JACKET PRINTED BY
CHENEY & SONS LIMITED
BANBURY, OXON

LITHOGRAPHY BY
BICESTER PHOTOLITHO LIMITED
BICESTER, ENGLAND

DISPLAY SET IN BASKERVILLE
AND TEXT SET IN 11/12pt BASKERVILLE
BY HARPER PHOTOTYPESETTERS LIMITED
NORTHAMPTON, ENGLAND

© Robin Bush 1983

ISBN 0 86023 186 0

CONTENTS

INTRODUCTION

I well remember the first day that I met Edward Jeboult. It was 26 January 1982 and I had driven over the border from Somerset into Devon to speak to an antique collectors' society near Axminster. Its members made up a large and appreciative audience and, over coffee afterwards, I was introduced to Mrs Constance Gray-Read. She in turn invited me back to her home at Chardstock to see two volumes compiled by her grandfather, Edward Jeboult of Taunton. From that chance encounter sprang this present work.

The first of Edward's two books was devoted to Taunton itself. In 1866 he had stuck newspaper articles which he had written on the town's history into a large album and set about illustrating them with some 500 pictures — engravings, maps, his own sketches, but most significantly with photographs which he himself had taken. Here, from the early days of photography, was Edward's own view of his natal town, peopled with scruffy urchins, girls in pinafore dresses, ladies in crinolines and gentlemen sporting 'stove-pipe' hats. There were long-demolished buildings, some of which I had never seen illustrated before, unrestored churches and chapels: a window into a mid-Victorian world which had vanished. Had this been all it would have been treasure indeed: but there was more.

The second book was Edward's lovingly assembled account of his own family: early 'cabinet' portraits dating from the 1850s, billheads, drawings of family homes, letters, anecdotes, marriage licences, gun licences, invitation cards and even school sports prize tickets; the compact, undigested, delightful story of the Jeboults as 19th century Taunton tradesmen.

That same evening, a generous whisky clutched carefully in one hand as I turned the pages, it was clear that there was a book here that cried out to be written. That it has been is due largely to the encouragement and support of a number of people and organisations.

Initially my thanks are due to Constance Gray-Read for so readily allowing the fruits of her grandfather's labours to be given a wider audience, and for the hospitality which she, her husband and her sister, Mrs Mercy Palmer, have so readily and regularly shown me.

Next, my gratitude goes to Taunton's reborn Civic Society and its secretary, Joan Viveash, which mounted the exhibition that popularised the collection, to the Brewhouse Theatre and its former manager, Chris Durham, who provided a temporary home for the photographs, and to all those whose consumption of quiche and salad was disrupted by interested Tauntonians peering across them at pictorial Victoriana. In turn, the exhibition would not have been possible but for the photographic skills of Peter Birch and the generous support by Mrs Val Stephens of Somerset's Museum Education Service. My thanks also go to Robert Dunning for certain details relating to the history of Hatcher's.

The County Librarian, Mr Roger Stoakley, and his staff, particularly Joan Stevens, David Bromwich and Bryan McEnroe, have once again been unstinting in providing subscription facilities, advice and help in almost equal quantities, not to mention understanding in the matter of overdue library books. I am also grateful to the County Archivist, Derek Shorrocks, for hardly flinching as literally hundreds of letters reserving copies of the book poured daily through the letter box at Somerset Record Office. Without the help of members of the Press the launching of the book would have been a much more protracted exercise, and I feel bound to mention individually Mr Kenneth Burge, the editor in chief of the *Somerset County Gazette*, Ray Stokes of the *Bristol Evening Post*, Martin Carter of the *Western Daily Press* and Norman Thompson of Beason News Pix.

As always my publisher, Clive Birch, has been a tower of strength — even to the extent of surrendering a sizeable slice of his Whitsun weekend to plan this, our fourth book together.

The text comprises a series of essays on the Jeboult family and the 19th century town that Edward would have known. It is not intended to be a comprehensive history of the town during this period, but is designed to complement the information given in my *Book of Taunton* (1977) and Edward's exquisite pictures. I have also frankly indulged myself on topics unlikely to be treated in detail elsewhere, such as the development of the Temperance movement and the Early Closing Association.

And finally my thanks go to the man without whom, as they say, none of this would have been possible: Edward Jeboult. We have shared an abiding affection for the town which gave him birth and which has provided me with a home for sixteen happy years. I can only hope that I have done him justice.

HAYGRASS HOUSE,   July 1983
TAUNTON

DEDICATION

For my son, Alexander.

LEFT: Mrs Harriett Jeboult (1789-1878), daughter of James and
Margaret Pounsbery, Edward's mother; RIGHT: James Jeboult
(1791-1858), china and glass dealer, chairman of the Local Board of
Health, churchwarden of St Mary's, Edward's father; CENTRE: a
Jeboult innkeeper from the *Salisbury Journal,* 1769; BELOW: Edward
Jeboult's signature from his book of Taunton photographs.

Edward Jeboult
Taunton
1866

PRIVATE LIVES

The Jeboults came to Taunton shortly before 1784. William Jeboult had been born at Salisbury in 1758 and trained as an organist under Parry of Salisbury Cathedral. He moved to St Cuthbert's Wells and, in 1781, to North Petherton, where he taught music and tuned harpsichords and pianos. By January 1784 he had arrived in Taunton where, at Mr Viney's, he taught the townsfolk to play the harpsichord and guitar. He was accompanied by his wife, Ann, with whom, according to family tradition, he had eloped.

The story is not an unlikely one as Ann came of a surprisingly well-to-do family to link herself with a humble music master. She was the daughter of George Layng, a prominent Wells gentleman and Registrar of the diocese, and her grandfather had been Henry Layng, archdeacon of Wells. Her grandmother was the daughter of the Wells Cathedral precentor and composer, Robert Creighton (c1639-1734), and granddaughter of Bishop Robert Creighton of Wells (1593-1672), personal friend of Charles II in exile. The later Jeboults were proud of this connection and ascribed to it their love of music, although none of the Creighton or Layng blood flowed in their veins, for William's and Ann's marriage proved childless.

To fill this gap in their lives William sent for his nephew, James Jeboult from Wiltshire. William's brother John, a boot and last tree maker, plied his trade at Salisbury, Fordingbridge and finally at Downton, where he died in 1836. His son James had been born at Salisbury in 1791 and came to Taunton to be trained by his uncle as a musician. Unfortunately he showed no talent for music and eventually joined his aunt, who had taken over Broomhall's china and glass business at 18 Fore Street on the corner of Hunts Court (now Bath Place).

William's music business flourished despite an embarrassing incident soon after his arrival in the town. A grand concert which he had organised at the Parade Assembly Rooms in the Market House in August 1784, with performers from Salisbury and Exeter, had to be cancelled when the colonel of the Somerset Militia forbade his French horns to take part. He went on to become the first resident of Hammet Street and for at least three years from 1805 he staged September music festivals in aid of the Wiveliscombe Public Dispensary. With prosperity came a larger house. William bought a site at Wilton on the corner of Middle Way and Fons George, and by 1814 had built a grand house which he christened, most appropriately, the French Horn. Later known as Hainesway House, the Jeboults let it in about 1855 to Major and Mrs Altham. For a week in 1856 it sheltered Mrs Altham's sister and her husband, the poets Elizabeth Barrett Browning and her husband Robert.

William Jeboult died at Wilton in 1817 at the age of 58. His widow Ann returned to her native city of Wells, where she took up residence in the Vicars' Close, earning the nickname 'the Female Bishop' from the generous way in which she entertained the young Cathedral clergy. And there she died in March 1840 at the grand age of 79.

The china business at Hunts Court corner was carried on by young James Jeboult and in due course expanded. In 1814 he married Harriett Pounsbery, a 24-year-old girl, who lived with her farmer uncle at Blackpool or North Town House (now Lloyds Bank, 68 Station Road). His early marriage he excused by saying that 'young men were scarce, most having gone to Boney's Wars'. It was remembered how he arrived at St James's Church for the ceremony in a new dress coat with the gilt buttons still wrapped in tissue paper. They spent their honeymoon at Clavelshay Farm, North Petherton, and that same year James took over 2 Fore Street (now Curry's) and bought his brother John into partnership with him in the china shop. In 1827 he set up a pottery at Bridgwater 'for the manufacturing of salting and pickling pans, water pitchers, and all kinds of vessels for kitchen and domestic use'. He occupied the 18th century glass cone there as his kiln, moving thence in 1832 to Salmon Lane. He suffered a severe fire in 1837, his brother's management proved ineffectual, and in 1840 he moved the works to Taunton so that he could exercise greater personal control. He selected an area known as Soho in Tancred Street, where he converted the former Cox's iron foundry, subsequently known as Pottery Yard. Clay found in the area of the Union Workhouse at Trinity conveniently provided the raw material. Edward later recalled two of his father's wheelsmen or potters named Mears and Massey who, he said, earned enough in three days to get drunk for the rest of the week.

With success in business James felt himself free to involve himself in the public life of his church, St Mary Magdalene, and of his town. In 1824 when churchwarden, he effectively countered popular opposition to the removal of the Crown gallery across the chancel for which a faculty had been granted by the Bishop. James secretly engaged a gang of workmen to meet him in Church Square at 4 am on a Monday morning without telling them why they were wanted. Within four hours the gallery was down and James had gone to ground while the parish erupted around him. Again as churchwarden of St Mary's in 1844 he participated in the great restoration under the vicar, Dr James Cottle.

On several occasions, in 1814, 1837-8 and 1841, the town was in danger of losing the Assizes for want of proper accommodation for the Judges at the Castle, and James offered the use of his own house and kitchen until better premises could be found. In 1839, following a spate of burglaries in the town, he supported the establishment of a night watch of the main streets, paid for by 6d a week which James and his son Edward collected from each occupier: and in 1840 a sergeant and nine policemen were duly dispatched on nightly patrol.

Throughout his life James was a staunch Tory and worked long and hard at successive elections. He was particularly prominent in the chaotic 1826 General Election when no fewer than six candidates contested the borough, following the retirement of the two sitting Liberals. On the return of two Tories his efforts on behalf of the second, Gen William Peachey, were rewarded by the presentation of a silver tea service, long treasured in the family.

With the formation of the Local Board of Health James was elected one of the first members in 1849, later serving as Chairman between 1855 and 1858. In fact he served Taunton almost until the end, for he suffered a stroke while speaking at one of St Mary's vestry meetings, which paralysed his right side and he died, after a protracted illness, on 16 January 1858 at the age of 65.

By his wife Harriett, James had eleven children between 1815 and 1835, all born and raised over the china shop at 2 Fore Street. James recalled how in 1815, the year of Waterloo, he took the news of the arrival of his first-born, Margaret, to the Pounsberys at North Town House in Station Road. Being kept waiting at the entrance he carved the baby's initials on the great gate, which long formed a reminder of his first venture into fatherhood. His first four children were all girls and James must almost have given up hope of a son when William arrived in 1822. James decided that there were better ways of earning a living than working in a china shop and apprenticed his eldest son to a draper, Robert Bunter, at the north corner of Fore and Hammet streets. Young William went on to work under drapers in London and Dublin before his father set him up in 1850 as a draper and outfitter, on a 21-year lease of 3 North Street back in Taunton. Tragically one of the town sewers at the rear of the premises led to William's illness and death before the shop had been open for twelve months.

The second son, Henry, followed in his father's footsteps, eventually opening highly successful china and glass emporia at Torquay, then Exeter and, finally, even in Taunton. Another son, George, was sickly from birth and died at the age of only 18 after helping in his father's Fore Street shop.

Of the seven daughters, one died in infancy and another, Mary, at the age of 19. The latter was a great letter writer on sacred subjects to her many friends, particularly Phoebe Handel, who later married Taunton timber merchant George Pollard. After her death in 1837 Rev James Cottle, then vicar of St James's, collected her letters, and two years later published them under the title *A Brief Memoir of the Life and Correspondence of a Young Disciple of Jesus*. Only two of the girls married, Ellen to an Exeter grocer, John Barter, and Harriett, who made a great catch by marrying William Rawlinson in 1840. Rawlinson was manager of one of the town's largest silk factories and Harriett's offspring gradually moved out of the Jeboult family orbit. Her son married a Yorkshire clergyman's daughter and two of the girls wedded surgeons.

James's success in business bought tuition for his fourth daughter, Susan, with a London artist, Miss M. Hucklebridge, who exhibited at the Royal Academy and at Suffolk Street, London, between 1837 and 1852. Susan returned to Taunton to teach the youth of the town 'water colour, pencil, chalk drawing and perspective'. She earned a local reputation as a miniature painter and as visiting art mistress to the Independent College (now Taunton School) and various other academies, dying unmarried at Teignmouth in 1888.

This work, however, is concerned principally with James's third son, Edward, born over the china shop on 22 February 1829. He was christened at St Mary's on 19 March when Mr and Mrs Joseph Henderson, hatters, stood as his godparents. He and the Hendersons' son were apparently two of the four Edwards born in the centre of Taunton in February that year, the others being Edward Clarke and Edward Parsons. As their mothers were all friends they agreed to celebrate the births of their four sons by naming them all alike.

Young Jeboult was educated at home until he was nearly ten, when James placed him, first at Clarke and Son's school, St James Street, then at Sutton's academy in Canon Street, and finally at Benjamin Frost's newly-founded Wellington Academy (now Wellington School). Edward remembered his Taunton childhood with affection. 'I was great at all rustic and country doings . . . no one around could climb a tree or find a bird's nest, could dive a dive or lead a gang as Edward Jeboult'. At Wellington he was captain in most sports, head boy of the school and carried off most of the prizes. This love of sport continued after he left Wellington — cricket, football, bowling, whist, and he 'was great at 5th November fireworks'. He loved horses and often rode with the Harriers, Foxhounds or Staghounds, earning the nickname of 'the Squire'. He claimed that his maxim was 'out last, home first, see all' but often he would return to town with the tired hounds at any time between six and midnight. In some ways his education and training fitted him more for the life of a country gentleman, but business called, and shortly before his 16th birthday his father took him away from school.

In January 1845 he was apprenticed until 21 to Robert Herniman, a well-known builder, contractor and surveyor in East Reach, James forking out the £100 premium. Herniman, however, gave up the building business in 1848 and the young apprentice served out his time with William Shewbrooks, a South Street builder, working on the new mansion of St Audries.

Edward might then have been expected to put into practice what he had learnt, but the untimely death of his brother William in April 1850, only three months after Edward had celebrated his majority, put paid to that. Instead James decided that the family investment in the outfitters shop, 'The Golden Fleece' (emblem of the Drapers' Company) at 3 North Street, had to be protected. An experiment with hired managers proved costly and Edward took over the premises for three years while his father looked for a buyer. Trade was depressed at the time but Edward made a success of the venture, and the store was sold in 1854 to another draper, Charles Whitrow Henderson. Henderson later succeeded to his brother's business at 35 Fore Street and closed 'The Golden Fleece'.

Edward was again left in search of a future. He found it at the hands of the Taunton and West of England Patent Manure Company, floated in February 1854 by a consortium headed by Dr William Edward Gillett, who ran a mental asylum at Fairwater House, Staplegrove, and later lived at St Paul's House. Edward was engaged as Clerk of the Works to superintend the building of extensive manure works on Kingston Road (used from 1868 by Hawkes and Spencer as an iron foundry and from 1876 to house Arnold's Rowbarton Brewery). The young man was paid 2 gns a week and later boasted that his skill saved the company £1,200. He followed this with a commission on Kingston House for J.H. Beadon. There he faced a strike among the masons which he quelled by 'reading the Riot Act' and giving the ringleader in charge until he apologised.

These experiences evidently gave him sufficient confidence to launch out on his own as a builder and contractor at North Town in 1855 'and soon had a large trade and many hands' — 60 by 1857. He built first three villas in Station Road: Arrandale and Sussex villas and Elgin Lodge. In 1856 he raised funds from his father, his brother-in-law, William Rawlinson, and others to buy the Cherry Grove estate at Rowbarton, which he sold off in building lots to increase his capital. He then acquired land on the west side of Cheddon Road on which he erected eleven model cottages, a development which he christened Sunny Bank. He also built rectories at Heathfield and Broomfield and was responsible for the restoration or rebuilding of churches at Cheddon Fitzpaine, Bishops Lydeard and Ashill.

He prospered sufficiently to fit out North Town Cottage in 1859 where he moved with his aunt, Mary Pounsbery, as housekeeper. One of his commissions was to erect a large structure at Pawlett within ten days to shelter those bidding for leases of Lord de Mauley's 2,000 acre estate there. Through Henry Smith, the agent at Pawlett Villa, he was introduced to Miss Dinah Hurman from Huntspill, a young lady 'of good education, manner and address'. Edward was immediately smitten, proposed and was accepted, but her father objected and the engagement was broken off. He next turned his attention to Caroline Brown of Torquay, whose sister had married his brother Henry, 'but all did not go so merrie as a marriage bell'. The lady had a former sweetheart whom she still appeared to favour. Although the day had already been named and preparations were well advanced, it was mutually agreed to break off the match. In the meantime the 'Belle of Huntspill' regretted her decision and reopened negotiations, but her elderly father 'raved and stormed' and again frightened her off.

Edward was not deterred. 'After a time the spring arrived, the birds mated and E.J. was again on the lookout'. As he himself wrote — third time lucky. His fancy finally lighted on a young lady he had known since she was a child, although there was thirteen years' difference in their ages — he 33, she 20. Henrietta Caroline Louisa Summerhayes — Hettie — was the daughter of a colourful Taunton personality, Samuel Summerhayes. Summerhayes was one of the leaders of the town's music, organist in turn at St Mary's, Wilton and Holy Trinity churches and bandmaster of the West Somerset Yeomanry Cavalry. Edward found his daughter of 'good disposition and temper' with a 'general bright and happy look'. His friend John Blizard praised her 'simple unaffected manner and her affectionate demeanour towards her father' which spoke 'volumes for the good of her heart in this age of frivolity and sickening affectation'.

The happy couple were united at St Mary's church on 11 June 1862 and honeymooned in London, Salisbury and Winchester, and Edward never regretted his choice. She did not seem to age as he did. In 1891 he could write that she, 'although looking a girl, is a grandmother'. Her family he never liked. On their marriage her father had agreed to insure Edward's life for £500 as her settlement, but he never did. Edward gave an account of the Summerhayes family in his scrapbook out of respect to his wife, 'but let it be known out of no respect to any other member of that family, for I hereby testify that I have none for any of them'. Between 1863 and 1880 Hettie presented him with a family of Victorian proportions, twelve children — nine boys and three girls. Two died in infancy and a third, the youngest, the first child to be christened at St Andrew's church in a font supplied by her father, suffered a fall on her head and remained a baby, dying in the County Asylum at Wells just seven days short of her ninth birthday.

With such a family it was fortunate that Edward's commercial life prospered. 'God be thanked, my business was always my pleasure, and it *was* business in those days; nearly £100 per week was turned — year after year'. But although his turnover was considerable he found little profit in building and grew disheartened with strikes among his workforce, so that 'when the babies came' he decided to look around for a more lucrative business. In June 1864 he gave a celebration dinner for his workmen at Sunny Bank and transferred to 46 North Street to become an ironmonger. There he established the Taunton Furnishing and Ironmongery Mart with a shop and showroom 200 ft long.

There was a time also for play. Having nearly drowned in the Tone as a boy, he headed a committee which in 1862 established a bathing place at French Weir. In 1865 he was elected secretary of the newly-formed Taunton Cricket Club and worked to prevent payments to umpires and players and to limit expenses to 5s per head per year.

Life as a mere retailer seems not to have suited him and in 1866 he took over Ann Creedy's shop at 48 High Street, and in due course added a marble mason's yard and business as a contractor at no 65. In 1870 he occupied 23 High Street and remained there for a further seven years. Edward never played as prominent a part in local government as had his father. Public office was limited to his holding in annual succession from 1862 the posts of High Constable, Portreeve and Alderman of North Street. In the first of these he set down for the first time the duties of Constable in a book that was used for years afterwards. As Portreeve he was bidden to collect the lord of the manor's rents and, on refusing, the clerk of the manor tried to secure the £18 Portreeve's money out of the market tolls. Edward forestalled him by giving the clerk one hour to surrender the money before he auctioned the clerk's furniture and thus freed future Portreeves from the duties of rent collection. As Alderman of North Street he revived the traditional tasks of keeping his ward free from vagrants and drunkards, requiring the public to assist him in the Queen's name wherever necessary.

In 1868 he was employed as temporary surveyor to the Taunton Turnpike Trust, although he lost the permanent appointment to William Easton by a small majority. He served the Turnpike trustees, Market trustees and Local Board of Health as contractor for many years. On one occasion he accused the surveyor of the last body of requiring bribes before awarding contracts, summonsed him and only withdrew from the prosecution following apologies and the intervention of the Master of the Freemasons. Despite strikes he persuaded his workmen to accept written rules of conduct, later adopted by all the builders in the town, who elected Edward chairman and secretary of their body. He was also responsible for some forty shop fronts in the town besides others as far afield as Cardiff, Manchester and Exeter.

Edward's services were regularly required for decorating the town on special occasions. He erected ornamental arches over the streets, planted temporary fir trees and fountains on the Parade and always made especial features of his shop and yard. In 1866, for instance, for the first flower show by the revived Horticultural Society, he designed a grand triumphal arch over the entrance to Vivary Park. It was flanked by the figures of Flora and Ceres with fruits, flowers and a sheaf of corn, all surmounted by the town arms.

The old china business at 2 Fore Street, in which most of Edward's sisters had worked, was finally closed in 1871. It had been carried on in the name of his mother, Harriett, who eventually died at her home, 19 the Crescent, in 1878. Edward's own commercial activities were briefly extended to Bristol in 1873 but after 'considerable sickness and loss' he removed in 1877 to new shops and workshops which he had built at Station Road in the garden of the old Pounsbery home. He renamed his business the West of England Stone and Marble Works and also began to specialise in rustic garden furniture. Also in 1877 he sought election as a Conservative councillor of the revived Corporation, but the new charter had been obtained through Liberal efforts and Edward was not returned.

Edward's last twenty years saw him continuing in business at Station Road, producing elaborate tombstones and timber gazebos, absorbed with his children and, as we shall see, with the history of the town. In 1890 he began to suffer from a spinal complaint which severely handicapped him. Thus it was one of his sons who, in March 1891, was minding the shop when Queen Victoria's second son, the Duke of Edinburgh, snowed up in Taunton for two days, visited the Station Road shop. The lad mistook the Prince and his retinue for a party of dealers on the look-out for bargains — even after HRH had departed with several choice pieces of china for 'some lady friends'. Edward loved to tell that story. Five months later he wrote that he was getting 'very doubled up and crippled'. Forced to take to his bed, he died on 17 June 1893 at the age of 61: if not exactly loved by his fellow Tauntonians, certainly respected.

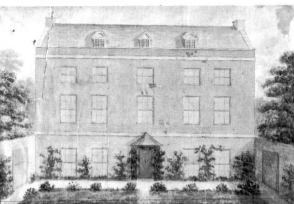

LEFT: Lectern presented to Wells Cathedral in 1660 by Dr Robert Creighton, Dean and later Bishop; RIGHT: James Jeboult advertises, 1828; BELOW: Blackpool, later North Town House, c1790, home of the Pounsbery family. Now Lloyd's Bank, Station Road.

ABOVE LEFT and RIGHT: Edward Jeboult's godparents, Mr and Mrs Joseph Henderson. ABOVE CENTRE: The Jeboult china shop at 2 Fore Street, next to Thomas Trudell's ironmongers. It was opened in 1814 and closed in 1871, and there Edward Jeboult was born in 1829; CENTRE: trade card of Susan Ann Jeboult (1821-88), Edward's sister; BELOW LEFT: Edward Jeboult aged 24, 1853. CENTRE: Edward Jeboult with his wife and sons, Charlie and Frank. 1865. RIGHT: Edward Jeboult, aged 54.

LEFT: Taunton Manure Works, Rowbarton, built 1854, for which Edward Jeboult served as Clerk of the Works; closed 1868; RIGHT: Hettie Jeboult, Edward's wife, aged 41, 1883; BELOW: drawing by Edward Jeboult of the houses he built at Sunny Bank, Cheddon Road, 1864.

J E B O U L T ' S
I R O N M O N G E R Y   W A R E H O U S E,
No. 46, North-street, Taunton.
EDWARD JEBOULT

BEGS TO NOTIFY THAT HE HAS OPENED THE ABOVE ESTABLISHMENT AS A FIRST-CLASS

I R O N M O N G E R Y   M A R T,
CUTLERY   STORE,   AND   BRUSH   WAREHOUSE;

And Laving, with Mr Trudell's assistance, lately selected a superior Stock of New Goods in the above line, from the best makers, will guarantee really good articles at extremely moderate prices.

The stock includes all materials in the Furnishing and Building Ironmongery, Grates and Ranges, Brushes, Cutlery, Electro-plated Forks, Spoons, Teapots, &c., Tools, Colours, Cords, Mats, Nails, Locks, Iron, Brass and Tin Goods, Shutes and Pipes, Sash Weights, Iron Castings, Washing-machines, Wringers, Knife-cleaners, and every Novelty, &c.

NOTICE.—At No. 46, North-street, Taunton, Gas, Water, and Bell Work, well-executed by experienced men in every branch. Repairs done with dispatch. In addition to the stock of Grates and Stoves, there will be found a very choice selection of Marble and other Chimney Pieces, of the lowest prices and newest design ; and in connection with the above, Tombs, Monuments, Headstones, Railings, &c., Designed and Manufactured as hitherto.

OBSERVE THE ADDRESS—

EDWARD JEBOULT'S Ironmongery Warehouse, Cutlery Store and Brush Mart, No. 46, North-street, Taunton.

ABOVE: Edward Jeboult's billhead, showing his premises at 46 North Street, c1864. Note the artistic license taken to include St Mary's tower; CENTRE: Edward Jeboult opens his ironmongery warehouse at 46 North Street in 1864; BELOW: Edward Jeboult's drawing of his building yard, High Street, c1875.

✖THE WEST OF ENGLAND STONE & MARBLE WORKS.✖

13, ✦STATION✦ROAD,
TAUNTON.

MONUMENTAL WORK
IN
GRANITE, MARBLE, OR STONE.

RAILINGS, KERB, &c.,
IN GREAT VARIETY,
AT ECONOMICAL PRICES.

GOOD WORKMANSHIP.
CORRECT DESIGNS.
WARRANTED MATERIALS

ANTIQUE OAK
FURNITURE.

PHOTOGRAPHS & PRICES
OF PRESENT STOCK
SENT FREE BY POST ON
APPLICATION.

SPECIAL
DESIGNS & ESTIMATES
IF DESIRED.

TERMS:—CASH.

ESTABLISHED A.D. 1854.

EDWARD JEBOULT,

Sole Proprietor of Capt. Clarke's Patent Firebrick Stoves and Fireplaces.

LEFT: Rustic furniture in Edward Jeboult's yard in High Street, c1875;
RIGHT: Edward Jeboult displaying his furniture, c1880; BELOW:
Edward Jeboult's trade card, c1877.

20

ABOVE: Edward Jeboult's trade card, c1880; CENTRE: Edward Jeboult's shop, Station Road, c1880, built in the garden of North Town House (left); LEFT: Samuel Summerhayes (1815-80), Edward Jeboult's father-in-law, in his uniform as bandmaster of the West Somerset Yeomanry Cavalry; CENTRE: John Blizard (1827-90), photographer, headmaster, Union workhouse master, and one of Edward Jeboult's closest friends. RIGHT: Cecilia Summerhayes, pianist, born 1840, married Alfred Anderson.

21

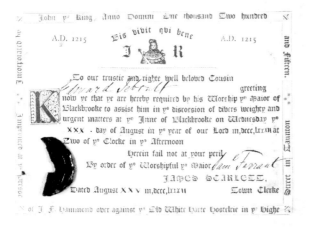

ABOVE: Interior of Edward Jeboult's works in Station Road, c1880; BELOW: invitation for Edward Jeboult to attend the Blackbrook Corporation at the Blackbrook Inn, 1882. James Scarlett, 'town clerk', was the landlord there. RIGHT: Cecilia Summerhayes, Edward Jeboult's sister-in-law, advertises her services with a commendation from (Sir) Charles Hallé.

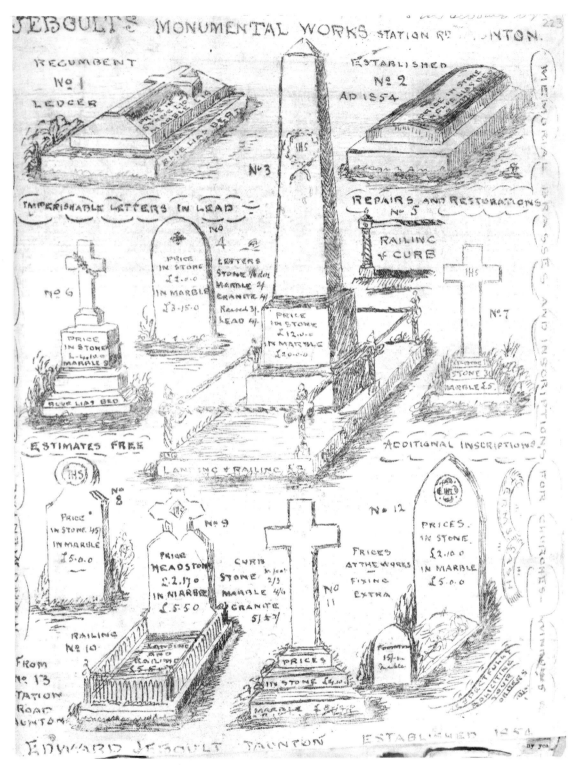

Price list for Edward Jeboult's tombstones, c1890.

ABOVE LEFT: Taunton Castle and garden, c1865; RIGHT: Taunton Castle from Castle Green, c1865; CENTRE: The Parade, c1865, before the Kinglake Cross was erected in 1867; BELOW LEFT: North Street looking north from a window of the Market House, c1865; RIGHT: East Gate, showing Gray's Almshouses (built 1635), c1865.

OF MEN AND MACHINES

The core of this book is a selection from some 500 photographs, drawings and prints of Taunton and its area taken and collected by Edward Jeboult within a few years of 1866. Edward's obituary in the *Somerset County Herald* makes it clear that the single volume of Taunton cuttings and pictures was only one of ten such books. Is it too much to hope that others may yet come to light? Even this small fraction of Edward's total output gives us a delightfully detailed insight into the topography and people of a rural mid-Victorian town. Such collections are rare, for few people were taking photographs in the 1860s, and those pictures have generally been destroyed. To find a collection deliberately and methodically assembled to portray the different facets of a single market town at such an early date is an incredible stroke of good fortune.

Photography came early to Taunton. In October 1839 Frederick Lake, an artist, jeweller and watchmaker of East Street, produced 'a daguerrotype or photogenic drawing' of St Mary's tower just two months after Louis Daguerre had revealed the secrets of his process in Paris. Lake's pioneering work was followed up in 1842, when John Young set up photographic apparatus, requiring an exposure of 10-15 seconds, in his nursery grounds in the area later occupied by the Elms estate in North Town. It seems to have been a shortlived venture, and there was little further photographic activity until 1851, when Mr Eastham opened a temporary studio at Robert Hellard's Temperance Hotel in Hammet Street.

The first man to make a commercial success of photography in the town was John Webber, who set up his business in 1853 and moved in 1857 to a large gallery at 52 East Street. The latter year also saw Edward Dyer, bookseller and printer, opening his own studio in Bath Place. By 1859 there were five professional photographers in the town, and by 1861 eight. Their numbers were increased by John Blizard.

A builder's son from Pershore, Blizard came to Taunton in 1849 as headmaster of St Mary's National (later Central) Schools in Church Square. He befriended Edward Jeboult and together they travelled to London for the Great Exhibition in 1851. They were probably among the 480 members of Taunton's Exhibition Club, which on 26 July journeyed by train to the capital *en masse* for a week of sightseeing. One wrote back: 'talk about Taunton, why it is not much larger than St Paul's'. There is no way to prove it, but it was quite possibly on this trip that the two young men, exposed to the wonders of 19th century science, became interested in photography. If not, it was almost certainly Blizard who introduced Jeboult to the hobby.

In 1864 Blizard threw up his schoolmaster's job and went into partnership with John Webber as a commercial photographer. Most of the early family portraits of the Jeboults were taken by Blizard or Webber, and by 1872 Blizard was practising on his own at 52 East Street. Later, in 1875, he was appointed Master of the Union Workhouse, a post which he held until his death in 1890 at the age of 63.

The earliest of Jeboult's surviving pictures are dated 1860 and soon after this his ironmongery trade cards were offering to send free photographs of his stock by post. It must be one of the earliest instances of the use of photography in advertising. It was, however, the combination of photography with Edward's other major interest, local history, which makes his legacy such an enduring one. In his work as a builder and contractor he occasionally came across relics of Taunton's past which he felt should be preserved, and these fired his curiosity. To him was due the discovery of pieces of the pre-Reformation rood screen and churchyard cross of St James's church and a pair of doors from Taunton Priory, and it was he who placed the crosses on the gable ends of the so-called 'Priory Barn', where they still remain.

Local history in Jeboult's day was more antiquarian than critical and Edward made little or no use of manuscript sources, relying on printed books, newspapers and pamphlets and, when these failed him, on the evidence of his own eyes, memory or hearsay. In the 1860s it was already 40 years since James Savage had published his revision of Joshua Toulmin's first Taunton history of 1791. Jeboult's only real rival in the field was Rev Thomas Hugo, an accomplished scholar, who produced histories of many Somerset monasteries, including an important work on Taunton Priory, and published accounts of St Margaret's Hospital and Hestercombe House. In later years, in 1877, Jeboult himself appealed for funds to publish Hugo's history of Taunton, but the necessary support was apparently not forthcoming.

Although in terms of scholarship Jeboult could not hold a candle to Hugo's work, between 1863 and 1865 he devoted himself to assembling material for a history of the town, and this he contributed piecemeal to the local press under the pseudonym of *Amator Patriae*. His motive was to make Taunton's history more widely known to 'the public at large' rather than see it buried in the published transactions of learned societies. By 1866 he felt his work to be complete and received permission from Lord Taunton to dedicate the book to his lordship, together with an advance order for five copies.

In the event he decided to widen the appeal of his work and add substantial sections on the history of West Somerset and the valley of the Tone, dedicated to the then Sheriff, F.M. Bisset, and the Bishop of Bath and Wells, Lord Arthur Hervey. He illustrated the work with 136 tiny 'heliotypes', the earliest known use of this process in the county, although for modern reproduction they cannot compare with his original paper prints. The book, of over 350 pages, appeared in January 1873, although less than 100 pages were devoted to his work on Taunton, and was an immediate success. He celebrated by naming his sixth son, born in May 1873, Arthur Somerset, although the baby died of whooping cough only two months later. Similar motives presumably led to his eighth son, born in 1878, being named Edward Taunton. Five hundred copies of the volume were eventually sold and in due course he prepared a second enlarged edition, illustrated with woodcuts rather than 'heliotypes'. He was preparing for its publication on the day before he died in 1893 and it was issued posthumously.

At the time Edward Jeboult appeared upon the scene, Taunton was a town of some 11,000 people, having doubled in size in the 30 years since the beginning of the century. It had not yet aspired to the dignity of Somerset's county town and was not officially to become such for over a century. In the words of Pigott's directory of 1830, Taunton 'extends from east to west about a mile, and consists of four principal streets, which are wide and airy, formed of good houses, and many very handsome; there are also other detached rows of buildings that may be termed elegant for their size — particularly the Crescent — which stand in an open and delightful situation'. To this Pigott might have added an almost total absence of sanitation, cramped backyard courts or colleges, unpleasant smells, a complete lack of corporate government, and a market that twice a week virtually closed off Taunton's centre.

When Edward was only thirteen the town was dragged forcibly into the 19th century by the arrival of the railway. The abortive Taunton Grand Western Railway Company of 1825 had given way to the more effective Bristol and Exeter. Until then the mail coaches had provided the town's links with the outside world, their very names giving a hint of magic to which only the wretched road surfaces gave the lie. To London, a mere 15 hours away, rattled the *Royal Mail*, the *North Devon* and the *Magnet*; to Bristol the *John O'Groat*, *Estafette* and *Nonpareil*; to Cheltenham the *Exquisite*; to Bath the *York House* and *White Hart*; to Minehead the *Diligence*, and to Weymouth the *Victoria*. For the transfer of heavy goods there were no fewer than 26 different firms of carriers providing regular contact with as many different towns and cities, the most prominent being Whitmash's with their waggon yards in North Street, journeying to London and all intermediate towns *en route* and to Barnstaple *via* Wellington, Tiverton and South Molton.

When the railway opened to Bridgwater in 1841, traffic through Taunton abruptly increased, as most stage coaches abandoned the Exeter to London route through Ilminster. New routes from Dulverton and Chard were introduced and coaches pounded through Taunton to Bridgwater 'to feed the iron-ribbed monster which threatens to devour their interests'. Their fears were amply justified. Within a few years coaches, one appropriately named the *Retaliator*, ran only to Bridport, Lyme, Minehead, Sherborne, Honiton, Sidmouth, Weymouth and Wiveliscombe, and many of these routes were to be threatened in the decades that followed. The town was never to be the same again. Tauntonians could marvel at a quarter-mile-long procession of carts laden with barrows and spades with which to arm the navvies, as the railway pressed on towards Wellington. At the site of the new Taunton Station the road to Kingston had been carved away to create the Rowbarton 'high path' and enable traffic to pass under the rail bridge. The first passenger train arrived 1 July 1842, and that night the engineer, a certain Mr I.K. Brunel, attended a grand celebration dinner at the newly-completed Great Western Hotel.

From May 1843 the line was opened as far as Beam Bridge beyond Wellington. For a year that tiny hamlet became the railhead, and attention moved away from Taunton, throwing a further 80 porters, ostlers and drivers out of work. The opening to Exeter exactly a year later came almost as an anticlimax for Taunton. A country girl standing on the Staplegrove Road railway bridge in 1843 and seeing her first steam train pass was heard to exclaim 'Good Lor! Good Lor! Well! As long as iver I live, they shall niver catch me goain by one o' thick there things, I'se sure!'.

The immediate effect of the railway on Taunton was mortally to wound the canal trade from Bridgwater and to transform North Town. That area had long been dominated by two major properties. Yarde House, an Elizabethan mansion of mediaeval foundation, stood where the northern arm of Wood Street now joins Bridge Street, and its grounds stretched west and south to the Tone. Flook House, of similar antiquity, possessed extensive grounds bounded by Station Road, Chip Lane and, to the north, the Canal. The lands attached to these houses suddenly became desirable. Yarde House, home of the Halliday family, was the first to go. Auctioned in 1846, it was swiftly demolished, the whole west side of Bridge Street was rapidly developed and Wood Street was laid out. The Metfords at Flook House were less susceptible. Initial building to accommodate the small army of railwaymen and clerks was limited to the north-western side of Station Road and the construction of Whitehall, named from land held there until the 16th century by the monastery of Whitehall at Ilchester. It was not until 1872 that the area of the present Albemarle and Belvedere roads was sold and laid out by James Culverwell Brown. The actual building was carried out piecemeal by a number of different contractors, much of the estate being exploited by local auctioneer, Walter Maynard, who bought nearly 3½ acres there from Brown in 1881.

The extension of the town in other directions also began in the 1840s. The area around the Sugar Loaf Inn, which was eventually to become Park Street, was sold for building in 1840, although the road itself was only constructed in 1847-8. Houses along the north side of Park Street were largely erected by Henry Davis (1811-92) of Billetfield House, including Cannsfield House (now the Corner House Hotel), completed in 1856. Davis was also responsible for house building at Billet Street, Cyprus Terrace, Haines Hill and Billetfield. He even designed his own coffin in advance. Working-class housing was developed also north-west and south-east of East Reach. Expansion was continuing at the time of Edward Jeboult's death in the areas of Belmont, Mount Nebo, Fons George, and on the Elms Nursery estate and in the vicinity of Friezehill, both off Staplegrove Road.

Edward himself reflected the Taunton of his time. It was a town of tradesmen, no longer dominated by a single estate or family since Taunton Deane manor had been gradually dismembered. It was ruled largely by the public meeting and kept informed by the public lecture. It was intensely religious and yet frequently profligate. It was above all a town of people; men like John Marshall of Belmont (1826-90), who gave generously but expected to be recognised for it, and who regularly headed a multitude of town organisations such as the Court Leet, the Gardeners' Society, the Conservatives, and the Bicycle, Athletic and Swimming Clubs.

At the other end of the financial scale were people like John Comer (1800-86), leader of the town's music, conductor of both the Madrigal and Philharmonic societies. He had been born at Bath and educated in Italy but in his latter years fell on hard times. He retired to Ilchester, where he was supported by gifts from friends and well-wishers and, on his death, an impressive memorial was erected over his Taunton grave by public subscription.

There were also men like William Brewer (1817-90), known as 'Billy the Piper' or 'the Wizard of the West'. By trade a pipe maker, he lived at 39 Alfred Street, where he also kept a small grocery shop, but he was known to a much wider public as a caster of spells and teller of fortunes. His funeral at St James's cemetery was obstructed by 'scandalous scenes' among the crowds who attended. It was a town of human and colourful characters, a town which thanks to the labours of Edward Jeboult we can still revisit nearly 120 years later.

Fore Street looking towards East Street, 1864.

ABOVE LEFT: Fore and East Streets looking east, 1863; RIGHT: St James Street before it was widened in 1866, from a drawing by Edward Jeboult; CENTRE: High Street, looking north, c1865; BELOW LEFT: girls with their hoops, at the top of Paul Street, c1865. The Memorial Hall on the right was opened in 1862; RIGHT: looking east up Middle Street, c1870.

ABOVE LEFT: Bath Place, formerly Hunts Court, c1865, looking west; RIGHT: Edward Jeboult's drawing of Castle Street, c1860, before it was widened. To the right the Winchester Arms; CENTRE LEFT: Gadds Court, East Reach, from a sketch by Edward Jeboult; RIGHT: south front of St Margaret's 'leper' hospital, c1865, used as an almshouse for West Monkton parish, BELOW: view down Shuttern to Upper High Street from the front of Shire Hall, showing right the County Gaol and, in the foreground, the Crimean cannon, c1865.

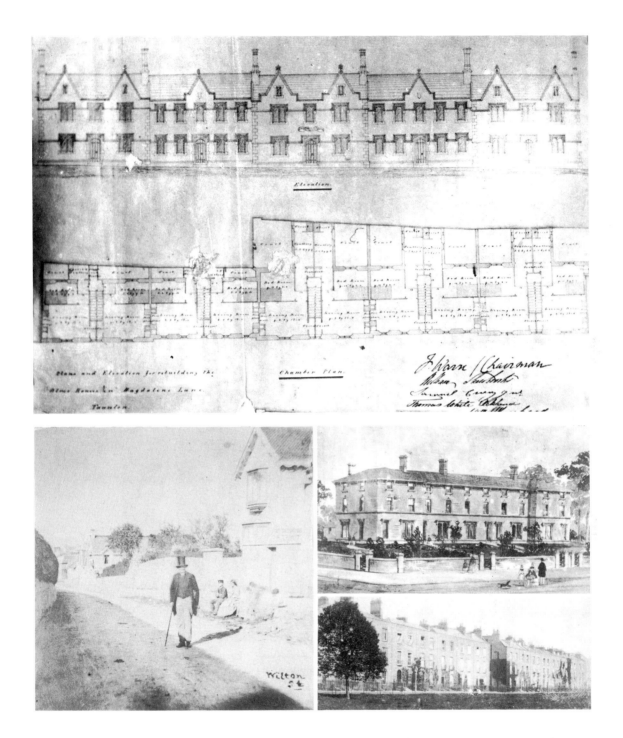

ABOVE: Architect's plans for the new Huish Almshouses, Magdalene Street, 1867; LEFT: Wilton Street, c1865; RIGHT: architect's drawing for Haines Hill Terrace; BELOW: The Crescent, c1865.

ABOVE: Afternoon siesta at Haines Hill, c1865; BELOW: Victorian grandeur at Haines Hill, c1865.

ABOVE LEFT: View of the former road to Exeter through an undeveloped Galmington, c1865; RIGHT: reflections at Obridge, c1865; CENTRE: ploughing in Hoveland fields below the walls of Belmont, 1864; BELOW LEFT: Hamlet of Galmington, c1865; RIGHT: Taunton Railway Station (Down Line), 1866.

ABOVE LEFT: Durston Junction near Taunton with the Railway Hotel on the right, c1865; RIGHT: view of the Bristol and Exeter Railway looking towards Bristol, c1865, probably in the area of Creech St Michael, showing the broad gauge line; CENTRE LEFT: West Somerset Mineral Railway, c1865, at the foot of the 'incline', showing *Rowcliffe,* one of its first engines; RIGHT: Watchet Station, c1865, before the West Somerset line was extended to Minehead (in 1874); BELOW LEFT: Trull Road, c1865. The stone walls were erected by J. E. Marshall of Belmont, 1860-61; RIGHT: bridge building at Thorn Falcon cutting on the Taunton to Chard line, opened 1866.

ABOVE LEFT: Cannsfield House, now the Corner House Hotel, built by Henry Davis in 1856, architect C. E. Giles; RIGHT: Lowlands, Trull Road, c1865 former home of Richard Carver, County Surveyor; CENTRE LEFT: Haines Hill, c1865; RIGHT: Elmfield House, c1865; BELOW LEFT: Mount Nebo as rebuilt by James Earnshaw Marshall, c1860. Following the death of his son, John Marshall, the estate was developed for building to designs by W. E. Roberts; RIGHT: Mount House, 1853; BELOW: St George's Villa, Wilton Street, 1865, occupied by John Donald.

ABOVE LEFT: Creechbarrow House, now the Creech Castle Hotel, c1865. Built by Capt George Beadon c1848; RIGHT: twin-screw steam boat, c1865, built by Capt George Beadon of Creechbarrow (1810-89), who invented the double hook, an improved lifebuoy and claimed to have devised the screw propeller; CENTRE: Haygrass House, c1870, occupied by Octavius Malet; BELOW: Hestercombe House, c1865, before its virtual rebuilding by the Portmans completed in 1875. Now the County Fire Headquarters.

FOUNDING FATHERS

For Edward Jeboult business was his pleasure; it put food in the mouths of his small army of children and eventually enabled him to devote himself to local history and photography. For Taunton too, trade and commerce were all-important. The very topography of the town centred on its thousand-year-old market place, the Parade. Over the centuries, however, its priorities had changed. The days when its flourishing cloth industry had dominated the labour market had gone, and in its place had come silk and lace manufacture.

At the time of Edward's birth there were no fewer than seven factories engaged in silk making or silk throwing, and two involved in the production of lace. The locations of all these were determined principally by the plentiful supply of water, mainly on the Pot Water from Vivary Park and along Winter's stream through Silver, Tancred, Canon and St James streets. Thus in 1830 the Pot Water powered George Stevenson's silk mills at Poolwall in Upper High Street, and Winter's stream supplied in quick succession John Jones's silk mill in White Lion Court (at the east end of East Street), the lace factories of William Cox and George Rawlinson in Tancred Street, John Parsons's silk mill in Canon Street and Thomas Atkins's silk and crêpe factory in St James Street. Elsewhere there were John Heudebourck's mills, moved shortly before from Barrack (now Mount) Street to Holway Lane (now South Street), William Blinkhorn's Backbridge mills near Staplegrove, in the area still known as Silk Mills, and Stokes and Sons' factory at Roughmoor in Bishops Hull. There had been six clothiers still in the town in 1796 together with a tucker and two cardmakers, but by Jeboult's day their trades had vanished.

The two lace works had both been erected in 1825 to emulate the success of Heathcote's mills at Tiverton, but they lasted less than a decade. Cox returned to his family's traditional trade of iron founding and Rawlinson converted his factory to silk production.

George Rawlinson had come originally from Leicester, where riots and machine breaking had driven his lace factories out of business. He moved to Tiverton to take over buildings in partnership with the Heathcotes, and then built his Tancred Street premises, the management of which he entrusted subsequently to his young son, William. When John Jones's silk factory closed abruptly in 1838, throwing 200 workers onto the street, George snapped it up and also took over the silk manufacturing business of Messrs James Pearsall of Cheapside, London. The production of both factories was then coordinated under William Rawlinson, who became Edward Jeboult's brother-in-law in 1840.

William Rawlinson was an intensely religious man, attached at first to St James's church and one of the chief movers in the building of Holy Trinity. His distaste for the Oxford Movement led him first to the Plymouth Brethren and finally to North Street Independent chapel, where he became a lifelong advocate of the Temperance movement. He was also prominently identified with the Taunton Town Mission, the Independent College and Taunton Hospital. Not all his good works were wholly appreciated, particularly the 15 ft high drinking fountain surmounted by a squat obelisk, which he placed in the middle of the road at East Gate in 1860. He tried to persuade the Board of Health to take it over but they described it as 'an abomination to architectural taste' and declined.

He retired from business in 1882, dying in 1903, his son, William George Rawlinson, becoming senior partner of Pearsall's, and the Taunton works being taken over by two former colleagues, Moses Stanway and William Summerfield. The company continues today under the revived name of James Pearsall.

Pearsall's may be the sole survivor of the industry which once dominated Taunton and, indeed, the manufacture was badly hit in 1828 by the importation of French silk, when many lost their jobs. The silk mills near Staplegrove, however, were not immediately thrown out of business. They had been converted from grist and former fulling mills by a silk throwster from Derbyshire, Isaac Hawkins, in 1802. Hawkins's son, John Isaac, later went on to become the inventor of the upright piano, but the mills were leased in 1803 to William Blinkhorn. He was followed in the 1840s by John Shipton (died 1850) and his widow, Catherine, and c1860 by Thomas Carter, under whom the premises were transformed into flaxmills, and later by Price Brothers from Wellington, who converted them into woollen mills, as they did in the 1870s with works at Rowbarton.

One of the oldest silk works was sited from the late 18th century in the former flour mills at Poolwall. From George Stevenson they passed in the 1840s to George Bloor and c1860 to Stephen Walters. By 1866 part of the mills had been taken over by the London firm of Young and Co to make linen collars, a manufacture which was eventually to replace silk as the staple of the town's industry. A similar change of use occurred in the silk factory of John Heudebourck in South Street, succeeded by his son-in-law, Charles Ballance. The works closed in the 1850s but in 1873 were taken over by W.B. Newland from Ilminster, renamed the Alma Street works, and also converted to producing paper and linen collars as at his existing premises at Ilminster and London. Part of the factory was bought up by R.M. Moody in 1875 for the same purpose, and he built the West of England Collar Manufactory at Viney Street in 1880. Construction of a 600-hand factory for the Cheddar Valley shirt and collar works started at East Street in 1881 and a year later Poolwall mills were occupied by the Taunton Manufacturing Co, producing shirts and collars.

Most of these factories employed female labour and, by 1882, there were over 500 'collar girls' in the town. Their morals were attacked in a letter to the *Somerset County Herald* which claimed them to be uncleanly, ungodly, bad, bold and profligate. The writer declared that 'they walk the streets at all times, and boastingly admit that what they lose by day in wages they can make up at night'. These accusations caused a furore. Henry Billet of the London Collarworks in Paul Street and Clement Smith, manager at Poolwall, leapt to the defence of their employees and the dispute even became a topic for Sunday sermons.

One short-lived collar factory was that established by John Goldsmith in the former St James's vicarage in 1886, which burned to the ground three years later, when the town's firemen were accused of being drunk. By 1888 there were nearly 1,500 collar workers and their numbers were increased by a new factory in South Street built in 1891 by Henry Van Trump. A farmer's son from North Petherton, he had started life as plain Henry Trump and evidently added the 'Van' to gain reflected glory from the 17th century Dutch admiral Van Tromp. He opened a pawnbroker's shop at 59 East Street, and it was probably insurance money after a £3,000 warehouse fire there which enabled him to go into manufacturing. He built a second factory at the north end of St Augustine Street in 1899, founded the Tone Valley Clothing Co, and went on to become one of Taunton's best known mayors, serving throughout the First World War.

In addition to collar and shirt manufacture, one man introduced gloving to the town. In 1857 Thomas Taylor from Stoke sub Hamdon built a glove factory in Wood Street, employing 300 hands in the town and a further 300 outworkers, and soon after moved into Weir Lodge. In 1889 the Tone burst its banks and Taylor's Wood Street factory was inundated. Vowing that he would never be flooded again, he built a larger factory on higher ground at Friezehill (Richmond Road). He used his glove-making profits to develop Bridge Street, Richmond Road and Albemarle Terrace, gave the land for Albemarle chapel, restored Mary Street chapel and, a lifelong Baptist and staunch Liberal, died in 1902.

Another family of building Baptists was that of the Pennys, timber merchants. Thomas Penny (1827-1906), born at Leicester, came to Taunton from Wellington in 1851 to work in the timber business of George Pollard. He laid the foundations for his later success when, in 1867, he obtained the contract to lay out the showground for the visit to Taunton of the Royal Agricultural Society. Subsequently, in 1876, he established his own timber business in a field in Wood Street and in 1885 bought the Greenway Farm estate. He and his son, Thomas Stubbs Penny (1854-1944) were responsible for developing the whole area of Rowbarton west of the Kingston Road. The streets that they built were named after Thomas's sons and grandsons (Cyril, Leslie, Raymond, Herbert, Thomas, William), Liberal statesmen (Rosebery, Asquith, Gladstone, Harcourt), and after Dr John Clifford, the great Baptist preacher (Clifford Avenue). One of their passionately-held beliefs was temperance, and to this day the area of their building activity boasts not one licensed house as a result of the restrictive covenants that they imposed on their purchasers.

One name still well-known in Taunton is that of the Goodlands, coal merchants. Like Van Trump they came from North Petherton, where for centuries they had been boatmen on the Parrett. Two sons of Edward Goodland, a farmer and celebrated wrestler from Moorland, settled in Taunton early in the 19th century. William Goodland (1797-1870) was appointed Inspector of the river by the Tone Conservators in 1826 and toll collector by the same body in 1830. In 1828 he established a coal business with a wharf in North Street and was advertising his Newport and stone coals a year later. His brother, Charles Goodland (1801-62), managed another North Street coal concern before setting up for himself at North Town Wharf. The two brothers later launched the firm of W. & C. Goodland at Tiverton but in Taunton they kept their businesses separate. It was not until 1891 that William's eighth son, also William, finally sold out to Charles Goodland and Sons, under which name the firm continues to trade.

Heavy industry in the town was limited to iron foundries. The oldest was that set up in 1810 by two brothers, Charles Cox, sergemaker, and William Cox, ironmonger, with William's son, William Charles Cox. They built their foundry in Tancred Street, whence they issued their penny tokens in 1812, a speculative venture which failed to pay off. Charles died in 1813 and William Charles Cox took over the business in 1824, moving the foundry, first to Fore Street, then to Tangier and finally back to Fore Street again. There it closed in the 1850s although continuing as an ironmongers into the next decade.

Cox's spawned another foundry in the person of their foreman, John Sainsbury, who established the Tone Bridge iron and brass foundry in 1816. On his death in 1855 it passed to his son-in-law, Cornelius Ash Lovell, and in the 1870s to Charles Allen and Son, in whose hands it lived out the century. A former partner of John Sainsbury, Joseph Savery, had erected his own foundry in North Street and Mill Lane by 1839 and William Savery had set up another in St James Street by 1848.

The largest foundry was that built by Walter William Easton at the end of Albemarle Street by 1882. Through the manufacture of generators the Whitehall Iron Works became the chief agency for the spread of electricity through the town. Under a succession of partners the business was known as Easton and Waldegrave, Easton and Bessemer and finally, by 1914, Easton and Johnson.

The importance of Winter's stream to the lace, silk and iron works to the north-east of the old borough has already been demonstrated. The plentiful supply of water also determined the location of two tanneries in Tancred Street. The older of the two had been started by 1772 by John Ackland, passing a year later into the hands of the Poole family of tanners from Over and Nether Stowey. Tom Poole of this family, for all his artisan background, became a close friend of Coleridge and Wordsworth during their Quantock sojourn. On the death of Tom Poole's uncle, Charles Poole, c1830, the premises passed in turn to Charles's brother-in-law, John Liddon, of a well-known Taunton medical family, and thence to Liddon's son-in-law, the barrister, John Alexander Kinglake. He sold out in 1845 to his tenant, Robert Parsons (died 1873), whose son operated it until 1888, when it was sold to J.J. Hayman, owner of another successful tannery at Holford. By 1896 he too had been bought out by Messrs French.

Joseph French (died 1824) was working as a fellmonger in East Reach by 1822. His son William (died 1844) continued the business in Tancred Street, adding a wool warehouse by 1839. His two sons, Edmund and William Charles (died 1891), extended their trade, describing themselves in 1875 as woolmerchants, fellmongers, and glove and gaiter manufacturers. Since the takeover of Hayman's tannery the company has continued until the present day, still under the names of the two brothers. They and their father were all Methodists and closely identified with the Temple Methodist chapel and Queen's College. As with those firms already described, they illustrate graphically how the trade of the town was largely concentrated in the hands of members of the Free churches.

One of the oldest firms in the town, in business throughout Jeboult's lifetime was Hatcher's, although known by a succession of former names. The concern dates back to 1788, when Matthew Colman set up as a linen draper next door to the London Inn (now the County Hotel), East Street. Requiring larger premises, he moved to a new house and shop opposite the Bell Inn at 12 High Street. In 1799 he sold out to Robert Newberry, a Somerset man from Winsham near Chard, but who had learned his trade at Holborn in London. Into the expanding store Newberry brought his sons-in-law, William Farrant (died 1848) from Wellington in 1819 and John Cook, and his own son, Robert Newberry junior, before himself retiring in 1827. When Cook left, another son-in-law, Rice Blake, came into the firm, and by 1851 his niece Catherine had married Demas Hatcher, one of her uncle's apprentices, who was eventually brought into the business as a partner. Newberry, Blake and Hatcher formally became Blake and Hatcher in 1865 and in the late 1860s and 1870s were showing profits which varied between £1,000 and £3,000 a year. A funeral service with hearse, coaches, palls, horse and waggon, Coburg and plumes, was introduced in 1869, and a furniture store had been added at 33 Fore Street by 1871. Henry and Robert Hatcher, sons of Demas (died 1892) and Catherine, entered the firm in 1876 and, following Rice Blake's retirement in 1883, the business became Hatcher's, as it has remained ever since. Its grand new premises at 54-55 High Street (now Argos) were opened in 1894 and the firm became a limited company in 1898.

A younger department store, 'the New General Drapery Establishment', was started on 8 March 1864 at 20 North Street by two Baptist brothers from London, William Muggleton Chapman (died 1922) and Arthur Allan Chapman (died 1925). They had a staff of 17 by 1871, and by 1872 had taken over nos 20, 21, 22 and 26 North Street. William moved away to Banbury in 1894 to found a similar business for his sons, and Arthur converted the store into a limited company almost simultaneously with Hatcher's in 1898. As Debenham's it continues to occupy the original although enlarged site.

A third store was launched personally by its creator, who well knew the value of advertisement. Thomas J. Lipton opened his 'great tea, butter and bacon market' at 22 Fore Street in 1890 following a lengthy procession of Turkish men under huge red and white umbrellas, all bearing placards proclaiming 'Lipton is Here!'

These are examples of three of the major business houses but there were literally hundreds of smaller ones. Robert Hellard, one of Edward Jeboult's rivals as an ironmonger at 23-24 North Street, was also well known locally as an inventor of agricultural machinery. In 1866 he was demonstrating his Self-Acting Patent Side Delivery Reaping machine which he proved could cut 15 acres of beans in two days without a single breakdown. There was Charles Fuge (died 1895) who supplied the Sheriffs' coaches from his works at 8 North Street and in Mill Lane, patented the Ina Landaulette, devised the Albemarle Cart, the Taunton Car and the Miniature Brougham, and succeeded a line of carriage builders traceable back to a Mr Reeves in 1758.

For a time Taunton sheltered a small colony of Italian jewellers and barometer makers. Among these were the Schalfino family from Como who later kept three different public houses in East Reach. Others were John Mazaritti, Peter Camarado, John de Maria and Peter Nolfi. A sixth was Joseph Amantius Butti, who arrived in Taunton in 1830 and married the daughter of the gardener at Silver Street Convent. He died of consumption in 1842, leaving his wife to become a staymaker and dressmaker in Silver Street. Of their children, Thomas was educated in Belgium, ordained in 1866 and became the first English subject to enter the restored Order of Franciscans in England, one daughter became a nun at the Silver Street Convent and another ended up as a Mother Superior in Dublin.

The small trader was also not afraid of fulsome advertisements. This was how F. Sharp of the Tea Exchange, 12 North Street, set about marketing his product in 1866. 'It is generally believed that the moral reform and social improvement for which the present age is remarkable, have had their basis in tea. The bulk of mankind . . . require something in the nature of a stimulant. Wherever this stimulant is tea, there is to be found the Spirit of Civilization in full activity. Where it is wanting or used in small quantities, barbarous manners are still predominant.'

One of the typical success stories of local tradesmen is that of John Steevens. Born at Stoke St Mary in 1810 and having served out his apprenticeship as a cabinet-maker, he set himself up in East Street in 1836. His talents were unquestioned, but two fortunate occurrences raised him above the common lot. The first was the cutting of Billet Street in 1847. As Steeven's rented premises stood on the north-east corner of the new thoroughfare he was forced to rebuild, and there arose at 64 East Street a superb, if plain, Victorian emporium backed by workshops and warehousing. With the increase in custom and capacity that these extensions brought, he was employing 33 men and four women by 1851 and could tackle an even more challenging project. For the Great Exhibition of that year he was able to plan and execute an elaborate piece of furniture which he christened the Taunton Cabinet, representing the four seasons and their fruits.. It attracted considerable attention in the Crystal Palace, was optimistically valued at 1,000 gns and the United States Commissioner even offered to defray the costs of exhibiting it in America. Locally there was some dissension when William Perry, one of Steevens's workmen, claimed to have designed substantial parts of the cabinet and in a huff went off and himself carved the Taunton Vase for the same exhibition. Short of funds, Perry ended up by having to raffle it. Not to be outdone, one of the town's fairer sex, Miss Kingsbury, triumphantly knitted the Taunton Bouquet, also dispatched to London. Only one of these three works, the original cabinet, is known to survive — in the County Museum.

Steevens went on to carve the Taunton Sideboard in 1862 for the International Exhibition in London, although its fate is unknown. Subsequently he added the profession of estate agent to his other accomplishments, and in 1866 gave a grand supper to 50 of his workmen in his East Street premises to celebrate the coming of age of his youngest son, Arthur. When John Steevens died in 1876 it was Arthur who succeeded him. The son converted the business into a general furniture store, adding departments for carpets and china as well as the trade of a licensed valuer. In 1879, among his other commissions, Arthur carved the mayoral chair for the new Corporation from an ancient oak tree found beneath the bed of the Tone. Indeed Arthur Steevens' name was to head the firm right up to the 1930s.

During the 19th century Taunton gradually became more of a service town, almost in preparation for its more full-blooded role in the 20th century. Banking played a vital part in that transition. The town's first bank had been formed in 1776 by Matthew Brickdale of the Court House, West Monkton, Thomas Darch and Edmund Trowbridge Halliday of Yarde House, but ceased payment in 1816.

By the time of Edward Jeboult's birth there were four banks in Taunton. The oldest, Kinglake and Poole on the west side of Fore Street, had been founded in 1790 by Sir Benjamin Hammet with Messrs Jeffries, Woodforde and Buncombe, and was later linked with the Esdailes, London bankers who eventually inherited Cothelstone Manor from the Jeffries. The bank was taken over by Stuckey's in 1838 when the proprietors were Messrs Woodforde, Kinglake, Woodforde and Poole. The brothers John and Isaac Badcock, whose family hailed from Bampton in Devon, established their bank at 7 Fore Street in 1800, where it continued, although rebuilt in 1844, until swallowed up by Stuckey's in 1873. Stuckey's of Langport themselves had started a branch on the south side of Fore Street in 1823, and later moved into the former premises of Kinglake and Poole on the west side of Fore Street. In 1908 they erected the splendid building on the corner of Corporation Street, until recently occupied by the National Westminster Bank, just before they were themselves taken over by Parr's Bank in 1909.

The West Somerset Savings Bank was formed in North Street in 1817, following a public meeting at the Market House, chaired by Sir T.B. Lethbridge, and £500 was deposited on its first day of business. The trustees bought the old Full Moon inn by the entrance to Vivary Park and, having been remodelled by Richard Carver, the bank was moved thence in 1831 where, as the Trustee Savings Bank, it continues today.

A branch of the West of England and South Wales District Bank was opened on the north side of Hammet Street in June 1835, and moved in 1865 to a newly-completed building on the east side of Fore Street. Considerable distress was caused when the bank ceased payment in 1878 and was dissolved in 1880. Its premises were later occupied by the Somerset County Club and the site now forms part of Marks and Spencer. The Wilts and Dorset Bank opened soon after 1861 in Hammet Street and also moved in 1865 to purpose-built premises at 4 Fore Street. The building was later occupied by the Inland Revenue and since 1892 has been held by James Drayton's jewellers. The bank itself was eventually taken over by Lloyds.

Fox Brothers, Fowler & Co from Wellington opened a branch at 1 Hammet Street in 1879 and built a new bank there a year later, despoiling Sir Benjamin Hammet's original concept for ever. Only in old engravings and in photographs such as those taken by Edward Jeboult can the former symmetry of Hammet Street still be appreciated. The building of Lloyds Bank Chambers on the same site has since compounded the felony.

Taunton made one permanent contribution to banking through Thomas Fearncombe Chorley, whose invention of a new form of crossed cheque was adopted by leading banks in 1858.

Finally, we tend to take the (now partial) Thursday half-day closing in Taunton for granted, but it was a privilege almost as hard won as the vote. Until the 1860s it was quite usual for the town's shops to stay open until 8 or even 9 every evening except Sundays. In 1863 shop assistants vainly placarded the town urging ladies to shop before 6 pm to permit earlier closing, and two years later the Taunton Early Closing Association was organised, to give shop workers an hour extra each evening from 7 pm 'for relaxation'. Electing as their president Major Altham of Stoke Court, they arranged winter penny concerts in the Castle Hall for the shop assistants to attend. Most of them featured home-grown amateur performers, a local band, recitations and singing, although there were complaints of the 'loud cracking of nuts and flinging the shells about' by those in the gallery.

The workers behind the town's counters were not to be content with merely an extra hour in winter. In 1868 they persuaded the linen and woollen drapers of the town to shut at 5 pm on summer Thursdays. The released assistants promptly formed two Thursday evening cricket clubs and others left in droves on evening rail excursions to Watchet. The movement flourished for four years until the tradesmen rebelled and reverted to their former opening hours. Eventually it was Bridgwater's example that persuaded their employers to shut on Thursdays at 1 pm and, in response, the half-day sitting of the County Court was moved from Monday to Thursday. The oil merchants and ironmongers, even Edward Jeboult, agreed to shut at 5 pm and the booksellers and stationers also complied.

The movement was last revived in 1887 to press for Thursday afternoon closure, but it took a further five years, until April 1892, to win the tradesmen over — almost 30 years since the shop assistants had first agitated for a reduction in their six-day 72-hour working week.

ABOVE LEFT: William Rawlinson, silk manufacturer, Edward Jeboult's brother-in-law, died 1903 aged 90; RIGHT: William George Rawlinson, born 1840, silk manufacturer, Edward Jeboult's nephew. Taken by Webber & Blizard; CENTRE: granite fountain, East Gate, erected by William Rawlinson in 1860; BELOW LEFT: John Turle's, grocers, now the Tudor Tavern, and John Babb's, tailor and woollen drapers, 15-16 Fore Street, c1865; RIGHT: the Taunton Cabinet produced by John Steevens for the Great Exhibition, 1851. (Peter Birch, Somerset County Museum).

OPPOSITE ABOVE LEFT: The Taunton Sideboard, carved by John Steevens in 1862 for the International Exhibition, London; RIGHT: Wilts and Dorset Bank, 4 Fore Street, built 1865. Later occupied by the Inland Revenue and, since 1892, by Drayton's jewellers; CENTRE: West Somerset Savings Bank, c1865, former site of the Full Moon Inn. The premises were converted to house the bank (founded 1817) by Richard Carver in 1831; BELOW LEFT: Tone Bridge, looking north, 1864. On the right William Trood's Tone Bridge House; RIGHT: Tone Bridge from the west, immediately after the small island had been planted out and swans introduced by William Trood, manure manufacturer at Tone Bridge Wharf, in 1864; ABOVE LEFT: West of England and South Wales District Bank, Fore Street, built 1865. The bank had been founded in Hammet Street in 1835 and closed in 1878; RIGHT: south side of Fore Street from the east, c1860, showing Greenslade and Son's shop, wine and spirit merchants, auctioneers and surveyors, who continue as estate agents in Hammet Street. Grocer John Turle held the Tudor Tavern and the White Hart Hotel can be seen in the background; BELOW LEFT: nos 36 and 37, Fore Street, Evans and White, linen and woollen drapers, silk mercers, undertakers, etc, c1865.   RIGHT: east side of Fore Street, showing the junction with Hammet Street. The *Somerset County Herald* is advertising diaries for 1865.

ABOVE: Interior of West of England and South Wales District Bank, Fore Street, c1865; LEFT: west side of Fore Street showing the New Market, later the Victoria Rooms, and George Abraham's ironmongers shop; RIGHT: view down East Reach, c1865. The shop on the corner was occupied by Edwin Burrows, saddler and harness maker, who sold up in June 1866.

LEFT: Nos 64-66, High Street; RIGHT: Charles Lewis's West Somerset
Stores, c1875, now the Tudor Tavern. Frank Jeboult was apprenticed
here in 1879; BELOW: Charles George Hook's tea and coffee shop, at
the sign of the Teapot, Cheapside, c1890.

NORTH STREET, TAUNTON.

MR. EALES WHITE is requested by Mr. LING to SELL by ABSOLUTE AUCTION, in the Large Music Room, in North Street, a quantity of Household

FURNITURE,

also two Organs, a Seraphine, Bass and Kettle Drums, &c., Mr. Ling having relinquished these portions of the profession, devoting his particular attention to the music and piano-forte trade, tuning, &c. The Lodgings-Furniture will be sold, in consequence of Mr. Ling's removal to No. 45, Fore Street; at the same opportunity will be also sold some good Domestic Property belonging to a Gentleman who has sailed for America.

The Auction will include a very handsome assemblage of modern table glass; some Nankin china, (50 pieces,) and plated articles; range of dining tables; centre and breakfast ditto; window draperies; sideboard; sofalounge; American-cabriole; easy, garden and various chairs; pair of 20-inch globes, handsomely mounted; musical clock; Dutch and alarum ditto; camera; pair of protection pistols; Whatnot, Canterbury, inlaid work-table, book-case; desks; child's chairs; engravings; text labels and brackets, antlers, gas-burner, carpeting, wool mats; wheel lathe, with oak bed and chucks, &c.; lamps, flower baskets, garden roller, pair of large bellows, &c.; mahogany four-post, Arabian and sofa bedsteads; marble-top and other toilet glasses; mattresses; bath; wash stands and other bed-room furniture, nearly new; some kitchen requisites; knives and forks; steelyards; scales, and a variety of useful domestic articles.

The sale will take place on the above premises in North Street, on FRIDAY, the 19th instant; and in consequence of the number of lots the Auction will commence at half-past Eleven precisely. On view on the morning of sale from 9 o'clock.

Brewery, Taunton, May 3rd, 1854.

Staplegrove, near Taunton.

MESSRS. MAYNARD and SON will SELL by AUCTION, on FRIDAY, the 19th May inst., HOUSEHOLD FURNITURE, &c, the property of Mr. James Poole;

Comprising four-post, tent and stump bedsteads and furniture; feather beds; bolsters and pillows; flock ditto; mattrasses; blankets and sheets; quilts and counterpanes; dressing-tables; wash-stands and ware; toilet glass; bed-room carpeting and chairs; rosewood sofa tablch; maogany round table; Pembroke ditto; mahogany breakfast ditto; 2 lap oak ditto; 6 mahogany hair-seat chairs; 6 cane-seat chairs; American clock; mahogany secretaire and book-case; easy chair; window drapery; 8-day clock and case; fender and fire-irons; kitchen chairs; wine and other glasses; tea, china and dinner ware; metal coffee-pot; pictures; brass milk pans; copper and tin tea-kettles; boilers; saucepans; frying-pans; &c., &c.

The above may be viewed on the day of Sale, until Two o'clock, when the Auction will punctually commence.

The House to be Let, with immediate possession.

Dated Laburnum Cottage, Taunton, May 5th, 1854.

Laxworthy Farm, Enmore, near Bridgwater.

MESSRS. MAYNARD and SON have received instructions to SELL by AUCTION, on WEDNESDAY, the 24th of May instant, all the LIVE STOCK, Implements of Husbandry, Cider, Corn in Ground and Grass on the Farm, late the Property of Mr. Anthony Kidner, deceased.

Live Stock—10 capital ewes and lambs; four choice young barreners; two excellent three-years old heifers seven years old, warranted sound and good in harness; 1 strong grey draft horse, and 1 black ditto; 1 light waggon; 1 spring cart, nearly new, with patent axles; 2 capital carts; 2 timber carriages; 1 gig; 1 hand-cart; pair new wheels, arms and boxes; chaff-cutter, nearly new; sets of breeching and trace harness; a number of timber-dogs and chains; lot of oak, ash, elm and poplar plank; and about 200 good fir-poles.

The above may be viewed on the morning of Sale, until 12 o'clock, when the Auction will punctually commence.

Dated Laburnum Cottage, Taunton, April 27th, 1854.

CROYDON, OLD CLEEVE, SOMERSET.

TO be LET by TENDER, for a Term of 14 or 21 Years, from Michaelmas next, Tithe free "CROYDON HALL AND ESTATE," of 165 Acres of Rich Watered Meadow, Orchard, & Arable LAND,

The above Estate is situate in one of the most beautiful spots in the West of England, with a House suitable for a Family of the first class; commanding delightful views of hill and dale, and the sea, which is only about three miles distant. The whole of the Land is within a ring fence, and the quality is of the most productive character, and will be found to be in the highest state of cultivation.

Conditions may seen & Tenders to be sent to the Office of Messrs. MAYNARD & SON, Auctioneers, Land Agents, &c., &c., &c. Taunton

ABOVE LEFT: East side of Fore Street, c1865, showing premises on the corner of Hammet Street occupied by Robert Winter Gibbs & Co, linen drapers and silk mercers, next to the offices of the *Somerset County Herald*; BELOW: sale of furniture and musical instruments by Mr Eales White, and RIGHT: Messrs Maynard and Son offer livestock and property — all in *The Somerset County Gazette* of 15 May 1854.

ON THE SIDE OF THE ANGELS

Church and chapel dominated the life of Taunton in Edward Jeboult's day far more than they do today. Division between the two never led to bloodshed as it had done two centuries before, but each delighted in the discomfiture of a rival, often in rather unchristian fashion. It was a time when congregations vied with one another to build afresh or extend, to beautify with larger or more ornate stained glass windows, pulpits and schools. It was a period when many and varied religious societies flourished, responding to the call of missionary zeal, the demand for self improvement and education, or simply to stamp out addiction to the demon drink.

When it came to ornament, St Mary Magdalene, Taunton's mother church, had thousands of pounds lavished on its ancient building. In 1842 its vicar, Dr James Cottle, boldly ventured upon a major restoration. He offered personally to spend £3,000 on repewing and heating the church if the parish would spend little more than half that to make the structure sound. What vicar today would or indeed could make such an offer? The problem was that a church rate would have to be imposed in order to pay the parish's share, to which nonconformists and churchmen alike would have to contribute. This anomaly led to much bitterness whenever the question of church rates was raised to repair either of the town's two parish churches throughout Jeboult's life. Frequent polls of ratepayers were demanded which sometimes allowed such rates to be levied and at other times rejected them. Indeed in 1860, when Archdeacon Denison convened a pro-Church rate meeting, another body held a rival gathering, attracting mainly pupils from the Independent College (Taunton School).

In January 1843, when the condition of St Mary's had been found to be much worse than anticipated, a rate was only allowed by 460 votes to 313. At one point a local branch of the Church Rate Abolition Society was formed and it was something of a miracle that the restoration was ever completed. Funds were augmented by bazaars such as that held in May 1843 in the Market House Assembly Rooms. Texts autographed by William IV's widowed Queen were among the items for sale and £190 was raised. Cottle even went to the lengths of lowering the churchyard by some 3 ft to reduce dampness in the church. Hundreds of waggon loads of earth (and many fragmented coffins) wound their way to the Crescent Field, future site of Shire Hall, where they were used to fill in the valley over the Gaol Stream, which had been piped underground. Jeboult recalled that the earth was not packed down hard enough, which in 1891 led to the swallowing up of a horse peacefully grazing on the spot. It was also in the 1840s that paths were laid out in the churchyard and trees planted, all under the watchful eye of James Jeboult, as one of the three churchwardens between 1842 and 1847.

Cottle's strength of character not only achieved improvement for his church but also landed him in hot water. In 1845 the churchwarden, Henry Turle, had to be bound over to keep the peace after threatening to horsewhip the vicar in a disagreement over ringing the church bells. In the same year the sexton, Stephen Charles Parkhouse, forbidden by Cottle to receive his customary tips, took his case to the Bishop for arbitration. In 1846 there were still £2,000 owing on the restoration fund and when, in 1847, the major part of the congregation walked out before Cottle's sermon because he had voted Liberal, allegedly against his election promise to the Tory candidate, it was the last straw. It came as little surprise to the parish when Cottle resigned only two years later.

His successor, Rev Henry Parr, a worthy preacher, had to cope with the next crisis: the rebuilding of the tower. The fact that the structure was unsafe was realised as early as 1853. At first the parish decided to mortgage the church rates for £3,525 to pay for the cost of repairs: In December, however, the diocesan architect, Benjamin Ferrey, recommended demolition and rebuilding, stating that 'the stones appear to be thrown in without any reference to bond whatever, and the mortar is entirely wanting in adhesive properties'. Taunton architect, C.E. Giles, put in an estimate for an astronomical £6,585 and in July 1854 a poll for a church rate rejected it by 480 votes to 99. Seemingly perpetual squabbles and all too slender public subscriptions continued for a further four years, and it was not until April 1858 that the old tower was finally dismantled. Beneath one of the pinnacles was found a copper plate inscribed 'John Foy, plummer and brazzer in Taunton, June 26 1745, aged 27 years' and an ancient trowel was discovered embedded in one wall. The obligatory bazaar was held at Shire Hall in 1859 and featured items lent by Queen Victoria and drawings by Gainsborough.

The foundation stone was laid by Col Charles Kemys Kemys Tynte on 3 August 1858 and the newly-arrived Sebastopol cannon, later sited in front of Shire Hall, was fired off in Vivary Park. The labour of hauling the stones up the face of the rising tower was entrusted by the builder, Henry Davis, to a donkey which, towards the end of its labours, had to walk almost the full length of Hammet Street to complete its task. Traditionally, when the tower was finished the workmen hauled the beast to the top and paraded it round to 'enjoy the view'. A public subscription ensured that the donkey was retired with honour and an alley way near its final resting place on the Mount was long known as Donkey Lane. Completion of the tower was delayed by a masons' strike in 1859, aggravated when blackleg labour was brought in from Scotland. The new tower of 153 ft was finally inaugurated on 8 September 1862 with a procession, service and a grand dinner for 300 in Meetens' London Hotel Assembly Rooms. The town was lavishly decorated and Edward Jeboult filled his window with a model of the tower and, as a builder, the immodest slogan 'Our art over all'.

In 1859, before the tower was finished, Rev William Robinson Clark presented himself to the vacant living of St Mary's, having bought the right to one presentation from Lord Ashburton. Such a practice was viewed by some as scandalous and at Wilton in 1888 led the Bishop to depose a new vicar, Rev Francis Dudley, who had behaved just as Clark had done. The parishioners, however, were too concerned with tower fund raising to bother themselves with querying the arrival of their new helmsman. Under Clark in 1862 St Mary's acquired a new vestry room in Paul Street, in exchange for the old parish workhouse in Church Square and Edward Jeboult in turn received a wife at Clark's hands. In 1863 the carillon of bells was restored and the first annual festival of parish choirs in the Taunton Deanery was held in the church. Since the later 1850s most of the rural churches had acquired harmoniums which duly displaced the old barrel organs, with a choice of 5-6 tunes, 'the squeaking clarionet, the whining fiddle and the groaning violincello'. Clark was also a firm believer in ritual and other of his changes met with determined opposition. The introduction of surplices for the choirmen was slipped through without difficulty in 1865 but the question of a new marble pulpit in 1866 was a different matter.

Today it seems incredible that a parish could be torn by dissension on such a relatively trivial subject, but to the Victorians it was a serious matter. The 'original' pulpit swept away by Dr Cottle's restoration, which later found a new home at Bradford-on-Tone, had been replaced by an unobjectionable one designed by Benjamin Ferrey. Ferrey now proposed a grander model and was supported by churchwarden Peter Taylor, who in 1864 had donated a new west window depicting the Last Judgement. What stuck in the throats of the parishioners was not only the unnecessary expense but also the series of statues designed for it which smacked of High-church ritual. Subscriptions were refused, church rates opposed (drapers W. & A. Chapman were among those summonsed for non-payment), protest meetings were held and the vicar's nominees as churchwardens were only narrowly returned in 1876. Eventually the pulpit was installed but, despite Ferrey's objections, with blank niches where the statues should have been set.

Such controversies had little or no effect on the impact of Clark's preaching, which attracted attention far beyond his parish, and his sermons were even occasionally heard within the hallowed walls of St Paul's Cathedral. In 1868 it became known that a northcountryman, Robert Horsfall had built St Margaret's church, Liverpool, and endowed the new living with a handsome stipend, solely to tempt Clark away to Merseyside. Clark even got as far as resigning from St Mary's. It also became known that Lord Ashburton had disposed of the advowson to buy a new yacht and that the patronage had fallen into evangelical hands. Some parishioners even clubbed together to buy a prefabricated wooden church, which they planned to erect at Billetfield and prepared to decamp from St Mary's. To solve their dilemma the vestry persuaded Lord Ashburton to assign to Clark the great tithes (which the noble lord had retained), so increasing his stipend from £550 to £820 a year, thus making Clark the only rector that St Mary's has ever had. When Clark finally announced his decision to stay, the church bells were rung for the rest of the day. In disgust Horsfall sold his Liverpool church for a Roman Catholic convent.

In 1870 John Marshall, the 'squire' of Belmont, and Dr Edward Liddon contributed the lion's share of the cost of raising St Mary's chancel by 2 ft, heightening the four arches there and installing a new reredos (by G.E. Street). Unfortunately, when Clark added a low stone screen and fitted chancel gates, the old claws were unsheathed and the protest meetings restarted, the opposition apparently led by William Price Pinchard, a prominent Paul Street solicitor. Pinchard and his faction forced Clark to rip out the new chancel gates and then proposed their own candidate for churchwarden. After a further seven months' wrangling Clark eventually got his faculty for the gates. No doubt flushed with success and confident of support from the vestry, he then succeeded in getting the statues put back onto the pulpit, in 1871, and added the figure of St Mary Magdalene and other figures in all the nave niches for good measure. Pinchard's son protested but his proved to be a lone voice and the pulpit proudly boasts its statues to this day.

That was not the last of Clark's 'improvements'. The eagle lectern arrived in 1872, again courtesy of John Marshall, and in 1877 the chancel was restored and redecorated. The only discordant note was struck by the Press, which commented that a new picture of the Annunciation depicted the Virgin Mary as 'a sleepy middle-aged matron, rather annoyed than honoured by the intrusion of the angel'. Clark's final crosses had a more personal origin. In 1872 he had to announce that his curate, Rev John Higgins, had become a Roman Catholic, and in 1877 that his own wife had joined the Church of Rome after living for two years separated from her husband in France. The only relative ray of sunshine during his last years in Taunton was the marriage of his daughter to the son of Sir Henry Cole. The happy couple, according to custom, left for an Italian honeymoon to a shower of rice and old slippers, and 'a pot of boiling water on the doorstep'.

The desertion of Clark's wife to the 'opposition' proved the last straw for him and in 1880 he resigned, emigrating to Canada, where he became Professor of Morals and Ethics at Toronto University. A strike by the choir in 1882 and stained glass windows, heating, screens and doors to celebrate Queen Victoria's Golden Jubilee in 1887 were the responsibility of the next vicar, Samuel Adams, who came from Runcorn in search of 'a milder and more congenial climate' for the benefit of his family's health. To Prebendary Askwith, vicar 1887-1911, fell the unhappy duty of cancelling the usual midnight service on New Year's Eve 1892, because of persistent drunkenness and of conducting Edward Jeboult's funeral the following year.

St James's church underwent similar additions and restorations but without the prolonged strife shown at St Mary's. St James's tower was also rebuilt, between 1871 and 1875, with sandstone from Sampford Brett quarries given by Sir Alexander Acland Hood. After the reopening ceremony the Bishop dined at Pyrland Hall with Arthur Malet JP, and the parishioners sat down to a feast at the nearby Ring of Bells. A new chancel arose between 1884 and 1885.

The major problem thereafter was to rehouse the vicar. The old vicarage opposite the church had been spurned by several 19th century incumbents as being dilapidated, damp and small. Despite a protest petition from several hundred parishioners to the Archbishop of Canterbury and a resulting public enquiry, the old building was sold in 1886 to John Goldsmith, to become a collar factory. The vicar, Rev Godfrey Kingdon, lived outside his parish at Salisbury House at the top of Billet Street until a new vicarage was completed at Elm Grove in 1893.

The most colourful episode at St James's in Jeboult's time arose from the Chapman family, who served that parish as sextons through three generations from c1795. William Mattocks Chapman, the second of the Chapman sextons, managed to remain in office despite being presented to the Archdeacon for habitual drunkenness in 1856. His son John's wife, Elizabeth Chapman, also filled the posts of organist and choirmistress from 1861. Unfortunately, in 1883 the churchwardens decided that she was deaf and should be replaced. Without even informing her they appointed a successor, T.J. Dudeney, then organist at the Temple Methodist chapel and music teacher to Edward's son, Harold Jeboult. Despite a vestry resolution confirming Mrs Chapman in her position, the vicar demanded the organ keys from her, which she duly refused to surrender. On the following Sunday John Chapman, as sexton, let his wife into the church early that morning and she sat on the organ stool all day while Sunday lunch was passed into her through a window and Dudeney fumed impotently. Both Chapmans were hauled by the vicar before the borough magistrates for a 'riotous, violent and indecent act' but the charges were dismissed. The same performance was repeated on the next Sunday, although a constable, stationed at the back of the church to quell any demonstration, was not needed. The Archdeacon and Bishop were dragged in to save the day and advised buying Mrs Chapman off with £60 — which she promptly declined. In the event Dudeney had to return to the Temple and Mrs Chapman continued in her hard-won office until 1885. On her retirement, a public subscription raised £73 9s for her, so that she showed a profit of over £13 for her obstinacy. On her husband's death she succeeded him as female sexton and continued until her death in 1922: a truly indomitable Tauntonian.

Jeboult's time in the town also saw the building of three new parish churches. The first, Holy Trinity, designed by Richard Carver and completed in 1842, cost £7,000 and the life of a Bridgwater labourer, Redwood, killed in a fall from its uncompleted tower. At a dinner to celebrate its restoration in 1882 the vicar commented on the 'tasteless' architecture of his church and declared uncharitably that its architect 'deserved to be buried alive under its walls'. The other two churches were both due to the munificence of Rev Frederick Jeremiah Smith. In 1858 his 10-year-old son, Frederick John, laid the foundation stone of St John the Evangelist, Park Street, with a silver trowel. In 1880 the same trowel was used to lay the foundation stone of St Andrew's, Rowbarton, by Frederick John's son, Eustace, then aged only 3yrs 10mths. An iron church at Galmington was added in 1892, the gift of Miss Cleave of Haines Hill, the congregation having worshipped in the schoolroom there for several years.

As a churchman Edward Jeboult had less to do with the Free churches and chapels of the town. For them, as for the Anglicans, it was a time for building new chapels and restoring existing ones. It was not, however, a time without disagreements. At Paul's Meeting (now the United Reformed Church) it took three years of trial sermons from some 100 clergymen before the congregation there managed to agree on Rev W. Young as their new minister in 1868. In the same year Rev G.S. Reaney threw up his ministry at Silver Street Baptist Chapel and left to join the Independents. Even they proved unsatisfactory to him and in 1890 he was ordained into the Church of England by the Archbishop of Canterbury in person.

Schisms led to the building of two new chapels. At Paul's Meeting in 1843, a disagreement arose over whether non-communicants should be allowed to vote for their new minister. Such a seemingly minor dispute led part of the congregation to move to 20 the Crescent until a new chapel could be built to house them. The arrival of the railway in Taunton in 1842 had closed down Whitmash's waggon yard in North Street and provided a site for what became in 1844 the North Street Independent (later Congregational) chapel.

A similar division at Silver Street Baptist chapel decided thirteen of its worshippers on transferring to the Market House Assembly Rooms in 1874, while glove manufacturer Thomas Taylor of Weir Lodge provided a site on one of his building developments just off Station Road. In 1876 this became the Albemarle Baptist chapel, possibly named after the Earl of Albemarle, formerly private secretary to Lord John Russell when Russell was Prime Minister.

Such developments were not achieved without bitterness but they did not lead to the kind of violence which greeted the Salvation Army when it arrived in Taunton. In 1881 Wellington members of the Army visited the Bible Christian Ebenezer chapel in Magdalene Street. A crowd hundreds strong stoned the chapel windows and chased them onto the Parade, where over a thousand people had gathered. Within a year the Salvation Army had established barracks in Canon Street, but only by using the name of the Temperance Hall Committee as a subterfuge. In April 1883 the Salvation Army band led by 'Happy Harry' arrived in town for a week's mission. Their first meeting on the Parade was broken up by a crowd of 500 hurling rotten eggs and ripe oranges, and the rest of the mission was confined to the Victoria Rooms in Fore Street and Davies's Public Hall in Silver Street. By June, however, they could make their first march around the town from their new barracks in Eastbourne Road, although its windows were smashed in August by a gang of local roughs after a pitched battle near the Parade. It was many years before the persecution that the Army suffered during its early days here became just a memory, and before its unselfish message became acceptable to the town.

One cause that drew its supporters from all shades of religious opinion in the town was the battle against the bottle. The first formal move came in 1833, with the formation of the Taunton and West Somerset Temperance Society under the presidency of Dr Robert Kinglake. The movement gained pace rapidly. In 1841 teetotallers and Rechabites rallied on Castle Green but were soaked by rain and then subjected to a torrent of abuse from a crowd of drunken navvies employed in building the approaching railway. A Temperance Hall in St James Street was built that same year and, in 1842, Robert Hellard opened the doors of his Temperance Hotel at the corner of Hammet Street, now occupied by Lloyds Bank Chambers, joined in 1856 by Pavey's Commercial and Temperance Hotel at 34 Bridge Street, now the Myrtle Tree Inn. In 1848 it must have seemed to some that the Almighty was acting most unfairly in again using their favourite beverage to drive a teetotallers' fête from Vivary Park into the Public Hall in Bath Place. By 1863 the Taunton Total Abstinence Society was staging a grand fête and in 1866 within a single fortnight sponsored a visit from the agent of the National League and held their annual Christmas festival in the Castle Hall. It is not generally known that the Royal Ashton Hotel in Station Road started out in 1869 as the Ashton Temperance Hotel and Commercial Boarding House, named after its proprietress, Mrs Grace Ashton.

The tempo quickened in the 1870s. In 1874 'a public house without the drink', the British Workman opened at 28 High Street, inspired by its owner, Edward Jeboult's brother-in-law, William Rawlinson. Although the venture proved a failure, the abstainers tried again by launching the Taunton and West Somerset Coffee House Company in 1877 with a share capital of £5,000. The Company financed a refreshment stall in the Market from 1879 and a year later started a Coffee Tavern in Paul Street, which served 500 cups on its first day of operation. They followed this with the Taunton Coffee Hotel (later renamed King Alfred's Temperance Hotel), opened by the Bishop of Bath and Wells in the former Jeboult china shop at 2 Fore Street in 1881. It was a brave attempt. Penny tokens were distributed about the town which could be exchanged for refreshments at the two establishments.

Many were attracted within the walls of both coffee tavern and hotel, but to promote Taunton temperance as a limited company and expect it to show a profit for its shareholders was a fond hope indeed. At first the committee ran their premises through a manager, but when their trading continued to show a deficit, they leased them to him. The lessee had to add the trade of a fishmonger in order to make a living, and even so eventually went bankrupt.

More successful were the additional temperance societies that were formed. A local branch of the Good Templars was started, twice attracting the Grand Chief Templar of England, Joseph Malins of Birmingham, to address its members. In 1882 local corps of both the White and Blue Ribbon armies were set up, holding week-long missions in a large marquee in Vivary Park, at one of which over a thousand took the pledge. In September of that year the United Temperance societies of the town held a grand fête at the Athletic Grounds, featuring E.P. Weston, a famous temperance pedestrian, who succeeded in walking 50 miles in 10 hours and, as an encore, walked a quarter of a mile backwards. The fête was dominated by a huge balloon in the shape of the Zulu king Cetewayo, but was markedly less well attended than the Licensed Victuallers' rival fête on the same grounds a week before.

Every artifice was tried. From 1882 a Temperance Benefit Society, meeting at the Coffee Tavern, tried to rival the many friendly societies based on the various public houses. Each church and chapel founded its own Band of Hope (united in 1890), a fife and drum band was formed to head temperance processions and later a temperance choir to uplift meetings. Thomas Penny, the Blue Ribbon president, held a celebratory meeting in 1887 at the Temperance Hall, High Street, to commemorate his own Golden Jubilee as a total abstainer. Parliament was petitioned in favour of the Sunday closing of public houses, whereupon in 1888 the Licensed Victuallers responded with a similar petition against it 36 ft long.

The battle continued long after Edward Jeboult had sunk his last pint and was most successful in the early years of the present century, when the teetotallers persuaded the magistrates to close many of the public houses in the town. It is ironic that the only reason that Taunton's central Post Office stands where it does in North Street is because the Spread Eagle Inn, the former occupant of the site, was deemed surplus to Taunton's alcoholic requirements.

ABOVE LEFT: Interior of St Mary's, 1863, before the chancel was raised (1870), the pulpit replaced (1867) and when the pews still had their 'poppy heads'; RIGHT: St Mary's church looking down Hammet Street, c1865; BELOW: south porch of St Mary's taken in 1863 after the erection of new railings and carvings in niches;   RIGHT: wedding of St John Coventry JP and Mary Elizabeth Todd of Mount Terrace on 27 September 1860, while St Mary's tower was being rebuilt. A triumphal arch was specially erected; OPPOSITE: east side of the Parade and Hammet Street, c1860, while St Mary's tower was being rebuilt.

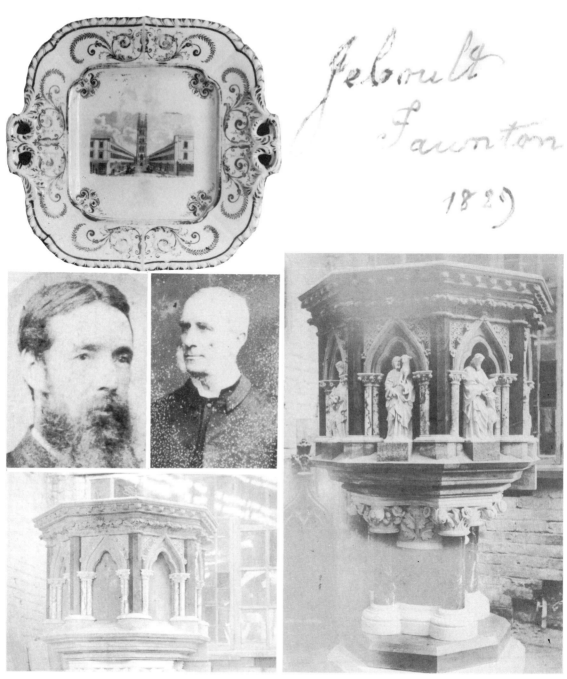

ABOVE LEFT: Plate produced by James Jeboult with illustration of Hammet Street and St Mary's church. On 8 November 1829 the collection at St Mary's was made 'in four handsome china plates presented by Mr James Jeboult with a commodious box for securing them';(Peter Birch, Somerset County Museum) RIGHT; inscription on the back on the Jeboult plate; (Peter Birch, Somerset County Museum) CENTRE LEFT: Preb William Robinson Clark, vicar of St Mary's 1859-80, (Rev R. F. Acworth) and RIGHT: Rev Samuel Adams, vicar of St Mary's 1880-87; (Rev R. F. Acworth) BELOW: Benjamin Ferrey's proposed pulpit for St Mary's, photographed both with and without its statues by John Blizard, in 1867. (Diocesan Records, Somerset Record Office).

LEFT: St Mary's vicarage, 1864; CENTRE: St Mary's Vestry Hall, Paul Street, built 1862, from a sketch by Edward Jeboult; RIGHT: mediaeval roof of the former St Mary's workhouse, Church Square. Demolished for the rebuilding of the Central Schools in 1866. From sketch by Alfred Alexander Clarke, artist of 53 North Street, 1851; BELOW: St James's church, c1865, before the tower was rebuilt.

ABOVE LEFT: Edward Jeboult's drawing of St James's vicarage opposite the church, sold in 1886 for a collar factory to John Goldsmith and destroyed by fire in 1889; RIGHT: the so-called 'Priory Barn', c1865, with the crosses which Edward Jeboult placed on its gables; CENTRE; view from the tower of St George's Catholic Church, c1870, while St James's was being rebuilt; BELOW LEFT: Holy Trinity church and schools, c1860; RIGHT: St George's church, Wilton, 1864.

ABOVE LEFT: St John's church from the west, c1865, while Park Street was still being built; RIGHT: Paul's Meeting, Paul Street, now United Reformed Church, c1865, before the present facade was erected and the building restored in 1877; CENTRE LEFT: burial ground in Tancred Street, site of the New Meeting, closed 1815 and demolished 1817, from a drawing by Edward Jeboult, 1860; RIGHT: Temple Methodist chapel, 1865, complete with Victorian family and perambulator. The chapel was virtually rebuilt 1867-69; BELOW: Bible Christian chapel, c1865, at south end of Canon Street, as rebuilt in 1864, architect Thomas Penny. It closed in 1935, was incorporated into Taunton Fire Station and demolished in 1969.

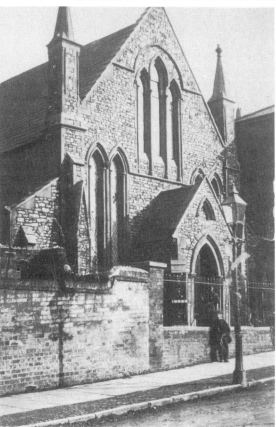

ABOVE LEFT: Silver Street Baptist chapel, c1865, before the present facade was added in 1870; RIGHT: Mary Street Unitarian chapel, c1865. The facade was rebuilt in 1881 when the two separate entrances were replaced by a central door; BELOW LEFT: Albemarle chapel (opened 1875), taken by Reginald Jeboult; RIGHT: Victoria Street Methodist chapel, c1865, built 1840, enlarged 1862, recently demolished.

PUBLIC AFFAIRS

The Taunton of Edward Jeboult's youth was a town without obvious leadership, for it had been nearly forty years since the town had lost its Mayor and Corporation. True, there was the Court Leet, the bailiffs of which acted as returning officers when parliamentary elections came round. The Constables' dinner gave Tauntonians an annual chance to celebrate, but the court itself had long had its teeth drawn. Its rhine ridders no longer cleared ditches and drains, its ale tasters no longer tested the local brew.

Apart from the county magistrates, the only active organ of local government was that of the Market Trust which, from 1768, had ruled the town market on the Parade with a rod of iron, although unable to prevent Taunton's centre virtually seizing up under the influx of animals and people. Not long before, in 1822, they had raised the classical facade of the New Market along the western side of the Parade. To this in 1854 they added a fish market on the site of the present electricity showrooms, the same year that butter at up to 18d a pound and corn at 9s a bushel led to a riot in the market. In 1840 they had tried to move the cattle market from Castle Green to Pugsley's Field at the eastern end of East Reach, but the transfer proved unpopular and the cattle returned. A further attempt on a site at Tangier proved just as unsuccessful in 1879. A new Corn Exchange, opened in 1868 in the former Fish Market, met initially with similar opposition. The farmers begrudged the 3d admission and the trustees were forced to drop the charge to 1d to break the farmers' boycott.

The trustees were empowered to prevent butchers' shops opening within a thousand yards of the Parade, and this was resented by the town's traders. One such shop was grudgingly permitted in 1835, but James Hardwill of 2 East Reach was determined to widen the breach in the market's monopoly. In 1869 he made his sixth appearance before the magistrates for illegally selling meat, and a public meeting in the Castle Hall persuaded the trustees to extend the number of shop licences to three.

The trustees also controlled the Market House, surmounted from 1831 by a superior clock given by one of the borough MPs and known after him as the Labouchere. The possession of this prominent clock and the advent of the railway timetable brought an end to Taunton time. On 19 January 1848 the Labouchere was finally put forward 12 mins 21 secs to agree with Greenwich Mean Time.

Another innovation made by the Market Trustees was street lighting; indeed it had been specified as one of their duties in their original Act of Parliament. The first forty oil lamps had been set up in the main streets in 1791 and the first demonstration of gas lighting was given in 1816 by East Reach plumber and engineer, John Wride. The company that he launched was wound up within a year, but its successor, formed in 1821, erected gas works in South Street on the site now occupied by the Eagle Tavern and successfully lit the town centre two years later. Oil gas gave way to coal gas in 1833, following the laying of new iron pipes throughout the Borough, after which the 104 workmen were entertained at the Phoenix Inn. The high price of the gas supplied resulted in public protest meetings and the starting of a rival company, which built new gas works at Tangier in 1845, their site still marked by a massive gas holder. The Market trustees, however, seem to have bitten off more than they could chew. Having spent £15,000 on lighting the town, they found themselves unable to pay their gas bill in 1848. The street lighting contract was the mainstay of the gas company and it could not afford to continue lighting the town without the cash in hand. Thus in November 1849 the lights were turned off for several months, plunging the town into darkness, under cover of which a spate of burglaries and robberies occurred. Eventually responsibility for lighting was reluctantly assumed by the Local Board of Health.

This new arm of local government had been suggested at a public meeting convened at the Castle Hall in 1847 by the Court Leet bailiffs. The townsfolk showed themselves particularly concerned at the state of Taunton's drainage, water supply and inadequate street lighting. Although commissioners visited the town to investigate plans drawn up by Richard Carver and Ralph Ham, the proposals were opposed by the Market Trust and by certain influential ratepayers, and the Bill was thrown out by a Select Committee of the House of Lords. Undeterred, the Bill's supporters, buoyed up by the passing of the Public Health Act in 1848, held further public meetings, and finally won the support of the Market Trust. In 1849 the first 21 members of Taunton's Local Board of Health were returned, William Beadon defeating Rev F.J. Smith as first chairman.

The Board's first concern was sewage disposal. In 1821 sewerage had been introduced to the town as a commercial venture by Taunton builder and brick-maker, James Lackington Rice. He had laid sewers under North, Fore, East and High streets and charged subscribers to drain into them, piping the effluent into the Tone near the bridge. This system never showed a profit for Rice although, for all its faults, it continued to operate until the election of the Board of Health. The Board concentrated first on those principal streets that lacked any main drainage: Silver, Canon and St James streets and East Reach. They bought out Rice's drain, as it was called, but the slow progress of the work led to harsh criticism of the Board, Beadon gave way to James Jeboult as chairman and several others resigned. As the work progressed, with Edward Jeboult employed as one of the contractors in 1857, more and more sewage poured into the Tone, which would formerly have been destined for cess pits. By the 1860s pollution of the Tone was reaching unacceptable levels. Effluent was piling up on Firepool and Bathpool weirs and Capt George Beadon at Creechbarrow House complained bitterly of the smell and danger to health.

The Board bought land at Obridge Gardens in 1868 to erect temporary treatment works while permanent works were being established at Target Field, Lambrook. Despite grim warnings from Dr H.J. Alford, it was 1877 before the Lambrook works were opened by the Mayor. The Fritz Hillé system of deodorization and precipitation which was adopted was not wholly successful and sewage continued occasionally to flood into the river. As the whole operation was imperfectly understood, the sewer gas sometimes collected at the works and, almost inevitably exploded, damaging the plant and endangering its staff. It was only after Jeboult's death that effective sewage treatment reached the town.

Next on the town's shopping list was an efficient water supply. The traditional sources of water had always been the Pot Water, which flowed from Vivary Park across the present Crescent car park, and Winter's Stream, taken from the Blackbrook and running through Silver, Tancred and Canon streets. By the 19th century both these were severely polluted by sewage and industrial waste and the pumps designed to augment them were little better. Yet again the public meeting was Taunton's way of forcing the issue, in 1856, although it was not the Board of Health that brought fresh water into town, but a private concern, the Taunton Waterworks Company. Thus the cost of the work was borne by investors and not the ratepayers. The new supply came from the Greensand formation on the Blackdown hills, six miles south-west of the town, with a small reservoir at Trull. The laying of mains was completed in July 1859 but demand always exceeded supply. The water was generally turned off at night, and whenever a fire broke out during the hours of darkness a long-suffering engineer had to be knocked up to turn it on again — usually far too late. The poor continued to rely on pumps and wells. The wells at Coal Orchard, at the bottom of East Reach and in Batt's Court were analysed by Dr H.J. Alford in 1874 and found 'to consist almost entirely of soakage from sewers and cess pools'. Alford declared them to be 'dangerous waters and quite unfit for domestic purposes', and went on to condemn Flook Well in Staplegrove Road. Eventually it was agreed to sell the waterworks to the Board of Health for £20,000 but, before the transaction could be completed, the Board itself had ceased to exist and Taunton had achieved its third Mayor and Corporation.

Since the town had lost its second charter in 1792 there had been intermittent attempts to secure a new grant. Petitions had been rejected in 1813 and 1815, and the majority of Tauntonians were apprehensive of the added rate-borne expenditure that a corporation might incur. William Beadon was howled down when he suggested a mayoralty in the 1840s, but Meyer Jacobs was more successful when a meeting was called in the London Hotel Assembly Rooms in November 1875. A petition signed by 1,708 was forwarded to the Privy Council, although another against the charter with 770 names followed closely on its heels. A Privy Council enquiry was held in 1876 and, the report being favourable, the new charter was granted in the following year. The Tories claimed that if the new Council took over the Local Board of Health and the Market Trust, it would start life with debts and pledges totalling nearly £65,000. In the event, although the Corporation absorbed the Board of Health, the Market Trust remained independent until 1926. The first election in 1877 returned 16 Liberals and only two Tories, the Liberals having been most active in obtaining the charter. It was 1886 before the Conservatives gained control.

The most significant development in the Corporation's early years was the introduction of electric light. As early as October 1878 the local YMCA had discussed the question 'will the electric light ever supersede gas as an illuminating agent?' and on 13 January 1879, to celebrate the opening of the Masonic Hall by the Earl of Caernarvon, electric light was first shown outside the Victoria Rooms on the Parade. Exactly a week later Taunton Rugby Club played Wellington by electric light near Wellington Station before a crowd of 1,200. Publicity for the new energy was maintained with a demonstration of Edison's electric pen at a bazaar in the Parade Assembly Rooms.

In 1882 Walter W. Easton's new Whitehall Foundry was lit by electricity where the British Electric Light Company established an agency. Easton offered to place two lamps on the Parade to show their efficiency, but the Market trustees declined. Easton was more successful in persuading the *Somerset County Herald* and *Taunton Courier* to light the exterior of their offices, evidently for advertising purposes. The later popularity of the light in Taunton was largely due not to Easton but to the work of Henry George Massingham, a boot and shoe maker and amateur physicist. In August 1884 he illuminated a musical fête at the Athletic (now County) Ground attended by 2,000. In December 1885 he got permission from the Market Trust to light the Parade for a month, and lectures were delivered at the Victoria Rooms. Among tradesmen who installed the light were W. & A. Chapman, linen drapers, and John Withycombe at the Castle Hotel. Massingham's demonstration proved so effective that on 1 May 1886 Taunton became the first town to have its streets permanently lit by electricity, powered by one of Easton and Waldegrave's steam generators. When in September the Castle Hotel lit its interior with Edison-Swann incandescent lamps, the chief surprise among its guests was that individual lights could be switched on and off. St James's church was first lit in the same month.

Following the 'conversion' of the Market trustees, the young Corporation agreed to replace their gas street lights with electric ones. Massingham received so many orders that he had to extend the lighting depot behind his Fore Street shop in 1882, and in 1889 removed it to the site of the old vicarage in St James Street. There in 1891 he staged the West of England and South Wales Electrical Engineering Exhibition for three months, opened by Field Marshal Sir J. Lintorn A. Simmons, former governor of Malta. It featured novelties such as Edison's phonograph playing a record of the band of the Coldstream Guards and an electrically-powered launch, which plied daily up and

63

down the Tone. Also linked with this period was the name of Francis Wheat Newton (1814-95) of Barton Grange, who built an electrical engineering works at Rowbarton to manufacture appliances popularised by the exhibition. Within a year the factory had its own works band and continued successfully until its closure in 1934.

Taunton Electric Light Co agreed in 1892 to sell out to the Corporation for £9,300, and Massingham opened 4-6 Bridge Street for the West of England Boot and Shoe Co, when his existing premises in Fore Street were taken over for the building of Corporation Street. Massingham eventually went bankrupt, became a food reformer and retired to Brighton, where he died in 1938. He was one of that band of unfortunate pioneers who made little or nothing from their labours.

The Market trustees, Board of Health and Corporation were the principal governors of the town in Jeboult's day, but there were other older authorities in the town. Taunton's roads were the responsibility of the Turnpike trustees, formed in 1752. The Trust's writ ran far beyond the town, as far as Milverton, Lydeard St Lawrence, Broomfield, Ashill, Fivehead, Thurloxton, Lyng, Trull, Sampford Arundel, Staple Fitzpaine and Churchstanton. The cost of improving and maintaining the roads, as elsewhere, was raised by the tolls taken at the turnpike gates and toll houses. Those at the time of Jeboult's boyhood were sited at Shuttern, Spittle (St Margaret's Hospital), the George Inn (Classic Cinema), Rowbarton, New Cross Lane (Holway Avenue), Holway and Newcastle (Cann Street?). In 1841 the George Inn gate was moved back to its former site at Friezehill (Staplegrove Road) and a new gate set up at the Crown and Sceptre in Station Road, later known as Cockpit gate. Any form of taxation was resented and, by 1843, Tauntonians had become fed up with having to pay for the privilege of going about their business. They petitioned the Justices at Quarter Sessions for the tollgates to be removed, but in vain. In 1850 Cockpit gate was removed back to Rowbarton, and in 1851 the Trust finally agreed to resite their gates outside the borough beyond the mile posts. Shuttern gate was transferred to Wild Oak Lane and Spittle gate to Halcon Corner, and in 1857 a new gate was built at Wheatleigh Cross, Trull Road. The last borough toll gate, in Silver Street, was replaced in 1861 by one at the entrance to Stoke Lane (now Stoke Road), and that at Friezehill by one at Cross Keys.

Tarmacadam was introduced as a road surface in 1831, replacing stones broken up into pieces of 1½ in diameter. New roads constructed by the Trust included Wellington New Road, bypassing Bishops Hull village, completed in 1838, and Park Street in 1848. The lower length of Staplegrove Road was raised by three feet in 1846 to drain away stagnant water, and in the same year Kelland's smithy was demolished in North Town to widen the road. Other improvements were privately financed: Alma Street by the Conservative Land Society and Haines Hill by Richard Carver and John Hare, both in 1858. The elaborate stone walling which lines the lower section of Trull Road was put up in 1860-61 by J.E. Marshall of Belmont as part of his projected rebuilding of Mount Nebo.

Improvements were not always executed without a clash between the various authorities. In 1862 the Turnpike Trust, in resurfacing the town roads, managed to bury ten fire hydrants just installed by the waterworks company. This can be paralleled by the Corporation's experience in 1883. They enthusiastically purchased a new steam roller at the Bath and West Show at Bridgwater, which not only proved too large to get into their yard, but also rolled out the new street gutters in Station Road on its first outing.

To keep down dust in the summer months the Board of Health purchased a fleet of water carts to spray the roads, and in 1862 three of these were seized by the Sheriff's officers for non-payment of rent by one of the Board's sub-contractors. The Turnpike Trust again had red faces in 1868 when their surveyor of 15 years' standing, John Leversedge, joint producer of a town map in 1849, absconded with Trust funds of over £270 and was never heard of again. The Trust was finally wound up in 1876, their toll houses and gates having been auctioned for only £336 the year before, and their responsibilities were transferred to the Highway Board.

Responsibility for the poor was taken over from the town parishes and, indeed, from those within a considerable distance of Taunton, by the Board of Guardians, first elected in 1836. The Union Workhouse, designed by Sampson Kempthorne, was not completed until 1838 because of the poor title to the land selected for the site. The Guardians also built a Registry house, designed by Richard Carver, in Middle Street, now known appropriately as Somerset House. The first Registry Office wedding took place there on 25 September 1837 between Charles Fouracre and Mary Riden.

The Workhouse itself was the scene of one of the most tragic episodes in Taunton's history. An epidemic of cholera hit England in 1849 and for several months it seemed that Taunton led a charmed life, although the dreaded disease came as close as Bridgwater and North Petherton. In September what was called a Day of National Humiliation was held in all Taunton churches, and thanksgivings for the town's deliverance were offered up at an open-air service on Castle Green attended by over 2,000 people. It was even suggested in October, when cholera broke out at Windsor, that the nuns might vacate the Convent in South Road to accommodate Queen Victoria and her household. Such feelings were unfortunately premature for, on 28 October, the disease was brought into the Workhouse by Caroline Hurby, a female tramp from Bridgwater, who died there four days later. In 18 days a total of 59 of the inmates died, including the schoolmaster but, although about 50 'healthy' paupers were evacuated to a house at Orchard Portman, the cholera was confined to the Workhouse and not a single case occurred in the town. Rev F.J. Smith, then vicar of Holy Trinity, took some 40 of the Workhouse children into Trinity School. The subsequent enquiry into the outbreak by Dr John Sutherland attacked the sanitary conditions at the Workhouse and the meagre diet. The tragedy had one lasting benefit. Those who died in the Workhouse could not be accommodated in St Mary's graveyard and St James's at first declined to take them. This led directly to the search for a public cemetery site, resolved in 1856 with the consecration of that on the north side of Wellington Road.

The Parade market, c1890, held there on Wednesdays and Saturdays until
1929.

ABOVE: North side of East Street, c1865, showing offices of the Local Board of Health (later known as the Old Council House). On left, James Larkin's, linen and woollen draper, at no 37; LEFT: Board of Health yard, Magdalene Street, from a drawing by Edward Jeboult; RIGHT: Shire Hall, showing the Russian Crimean War cannon, a 24-pounder, given to the town in 1857; BELOW: drawing by Edward Jeboult of the Taunton Gas Works built at Tangier in 1845. Note the flag on the gas holder.

ABOVE LEFT: Shire Hall from Shuttern; RIGHT: Taunton Union Workhouse, c1865, architect Sampson Kempthorne, completed 1838. The figure in the foreground is probably Peter Paltridge, the workhouse master; BELOW: Taunton Police Station, east of Shire Hall, c1865. It was built in 1856, extended in 1874 and demolished in 1963.

GENTLEMEN,

your Trust.   I thank you for the temporary appointment of Surveyor to

I now seek the permanent engagement, and beg the favour of your vote and interest at the Election on Tuesday next. *week*.

I trust the following may be considered suitable claims for the office :

Nearly twenty year's experience in the management of men, contracts, houses and materials, similar to those of your trust.

An intimate knowledge of your roads and property, and of all your proceedings for many years past.

And a conscientious desire to carry out the duties of the office in a complete and satisfactory manner.

Having made arrangements with Mr. Long (my foreman for the past fifteen years) to manage the labour department of my own business, I should be enabled to devote the greater part of my time to the duties of the Surveyorship, so that the work would not be done by proxy, or by clerks ; or from information supplied by the contractors themselves.

Having assorted all your papers and accounts in use for the past fifteen years, and having posted the whole of your books for the last six months, and occasionally assisted your late Surveyor, I am possessed of advantages which no other competitor enjoys.

I believe my Testimonials will be found second to none.

Should you be pleased to appoint me to the office, it would be my endeavour to render the roads and property of the Taunton Trust a model to the surrounding districts.

I have the honour to be, Gentlemen,

Yours obediently,

Taunton, June 26th, 1868.   EDWARD JEBOULT.

EXTRACTS from some of the Testimonials to be submitted to the Trustees on Tuesday, July 7th, 1868.

From the late Dr. GILLETT, of Fairwater, *in the year* 1854.

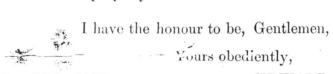

I have much pleasure in recommending Mr. EDWARD JEBOULT as an active, intelligent, and obliging person. He was engaged as Clerk of the works in superintending some extensive Buildings, in which he has shewn much ability, zeal, and unremitting attention ; and he has given great satisfaction to his employers.

Edward Jeboult vainly solicits the post of Turnpike Surveyor, in print!
(1868).

ABOVE: Invitation card to the Constable's Dinner when Edward Jeboult was constable, 1862; LEFT: one of the two mortuary chapels at the Wellington Road Cemetery, consecrated 1856; RIGHT: view in the Wellington Road Cemetery, c1870.

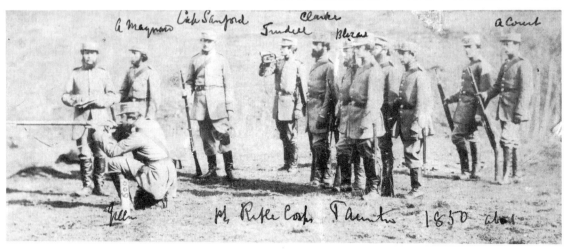

ABOVE: Facade of Taunton and Somerset Hospital, East Reach, c1865, opened in 1812 to celebrate George III's Golden Jubilee; LEFT: Taunton and Somerset Hospital from the south-east, c1865; RIGHT: design for the County Hospital; BELOW: Taunton Rifle Corps formed 1862. Among those shown was Edward Jeboult's friend, John Blizard.

A Little Learning

When Edward Jeboult reached school age his father dispatched him in quick succession to three private academies, the last at Wellington. In most towns a tradesman of James Jeboult's standing would have sent his son to the old endowed grammar school, but at Taunton the old College School, in what are now the Municipal Buildings, had been virtually moribund since before the beginning of the century.

Successive headmasters drew the small salary of £30 a year and educated a handful of boys in the classics for substantial fees. Efforts had been made to revive interest in the school at a public meeting in 1823, when Rev Thomas Forster was appointed. Following the death of his successor, Richard Winsloe of Mount Nebo House, in 1842, attempts were vainly made to establish a proprietary school. The next serious moves were made in 1855. Under Rev W.R. Crotch there had been no boarders and never more than five day boys. Crotch had enlarged the headmaster's house and claimed to have spent over £500 on the premises. The town saw only that Crotch, having lost his last two pupils, had locked up the school but continued to draw his salary. He was eventually persuaded to resign, although getting him to surrender the buildings proved more difficult.

Eventually the wealthy vicar of Holy Trinity, Rev F.J. Smith, was appointed titular headmaster. He accepted the post on condition that he should receive no salary, would oversee the general running of the school and undertake no teaching duties. The worker at the coal face was to be the under-master, Rev Joseph Mason Cox, who would receive £200 a year. He and the other assistant masters would take boarders in their own houses. The large dormitory which is now the Borough Council Chamber was formed by throwing several small rooms into one and, following a celebration dinner at Pattison's Castle Hotel, the school reopened in September 1855 with 20 pupils, a number which rose to 35 within a year. It proved a brave but vain attempt. Cox resigned after a mere four years and it was only with the resignation of his successor, Rev H.G. Heaven, that the school's fortunes took a turn for the better.

In 1864 Rev William Tuckwell became headmaster, backed by a guarantee fund of nearly £500 in case sufficient pupils did not enroll. Tuckwell proved to be one of those talented individuals who successfully transformed the classical education served up by the old grammar schools into a well-balanced general education, particularly in the fields of science and mathematics. To a dull curriculum he added chemistry, drawing, German, French, drama, drilling, boxing, gymnastics, cricket and football. A year later he erected a boat house on the Tone and launched three Oxford-built boats; he created a botanical garden, established a museum and a small observatory to take weather readings, and started a magazine of meteorology and natural history, *Eyes and No Eyes*. It was however clear that, on a constricted site in the centre of town, the school could never prosper. The nearest cricket field was a considerable distance away, the smells from the nearby Fish Market and public urinal, and the noise from the cattle and sheep markets and manor pound handicapped Tuckwell's vision.

In 1866 a committee selected the site for a new school in fields at Galmington south of the Wellington Road opposite the cemetery, and a limited company was launched to build it. At its head was Lord

Taunton, chairman also of the Schools Inquiry Commission. Disagreements with the landowner forced a switch in the intended site to the old racecourse on South Road, the foundation stone was laid by Lady Taunton in 1868 and the new school opened in 1870. Numbers had already been raised from 20 to 70 and, at its height, Tuckwell had 120 pupils, equal to the heady days of the early 18th century under James Upton. Unfortunately the seeds of decline were already apparent. The new buildings, planned to cost £8,000, had already eaten up over £12,000 and all the shares in the company running the school had not been taken up. The result was a heavy annual loan charge at a time when Tuckwell had lost the backing of Lord Taunton with his death in 1869. Tuckwell had also waived any religious qualification and thus allowed the sons of dissenters to enter the school for the first time, earning the enmity of the established clergy of the town. Even the personal endorsement of the Bishop could not counter the rumblings of discontent from Rev F. J. Smith, the former nominal headmaster, and Rev W. R. Clark, vicar of St Mary's. They hinted darkly that Tuckwell's religious teaching was unorthodox and that his politics were radical.

The inevitable result was that numbers began to decline. Two outbreaks of scarlet fever scared others away and in 1876 a mortgage of £3,000 was called in. Ironically Tuckwell's national reputation had never been higher. He spoke to the British Association at Edinburgh on science teaching and gave evidence to a Royal Commission on the subject. In a rash moment he promised to resign if the number of pupils in the school did not increase, and in 1877 the directors called upon him to honour that promise. He left to take up a housemastership at Blundell's School, Tiverton, and subsequently life as a humble although left-wing clergyman.

In his place came Rev Henry Pearse Knapton, who pledged himself 'to avoid party spirit in religious and political matters' and declared himself to be 'a Liberal Conservative and firm, but not extreme, churchman'. Financial affairs did not improve and numbers plummeted still further. In 1879 with a mortgage debt standing at £10,750 the school buildings were put up for auction and later sold for £8,000 to Canon Woodard to provide a home for King Alfred's (now King's) College, opened in 1880.

Like a dog with its tail between its legs the old College School slunk back into the town: first to the Victoria Rooms on the Parade with only 45 boys and then to its former home in the present Municipal Buildings. It staggered on for a further five years until Christmas 1885 when, with a mere 30 pupils, the Taunton College School Company was finally wound up. Bishop Fox's experiment of four and a half centuries before had come to a sad and rather ignominious end.

Tuckwell's efforts to woo the dissenters were not wholly inspired by educational impartiality. The great 19th century scholastic successes in the town were those of Queen's College, founded at Taunton Castle in 1843 as the Wesleyan Collegiate Institution, and Taunton School, started on Wellington Road as the West of England Dissenters Proprietary School, by the Independents in 1847. Both drew strength from popular nonconformist chapels in the town: the Temple and North Street Independent. The provision of extensive new buildings for these schools, which their supporters took care should be free of the weight of debt which had crushed the old College School, has ensured their survival to the present day.

James Jeboult, however, as a staunch churchman, sent his children elsewhere. The six girls all went to Mary Street, to the young ladies' academy run by the wife of William Chappell Ball, organist of St Mary's. Of the boys, William and Henry were sent to Thomas Simmons Crosswell, North Petherton, and then to Messrs Clarke and Son, St James Street. Edward also spent some time at Clarkes' and with George proceeded to Henry Sutton's in Canon Street. George Jeboult was 'finished' at George Rogers' Fullands School where, according to Edward, 'at the same time was General Gordon of the Soudan, who was allowed to perish by the carelessness and incompetence of the Prime Minister of England, W. E. Gladstone'.

Edward, like his father, started all his children off at private schools. Frank received his education at Caroline Whitwam's at 3 Mount Place and at Enoch Russell's at 1 St James Place, Middle Street. Charles Green and Charles Richard Russell had run Fullands School for Mrs Morse until she sold out to William Read in 1859. They had then set up their own 'Classical, Mathematical and Commercial School' at 48 East Street, and it was there that Charles completed his education. It was later taken over wholly by Charles Green, who moved it to 1 Albemarle Street in 1882.

Four of Edward's children were eventually sent to one of the Huish's schools, Taunton's great 19th century experiment in middle class education. Huish's Charity had been endowed by Richard Huish (died 1616) with fifteen houses in Blackfriars. Although destroyed in the Great Fire of London, their sites had rocketed in value by the 19th century. With the increased income, Huish's almshouses were rebuilt in Magdalene Street in 1867, but once the almsmen had been supported and West Country students at university maintained, there were no other legitimate demands on the charity's surplus funds. The Endowed School Commission proposed in 1871 that two middle class schools for both boys and girls should be established, and that these should be non-sectarian: open to nonconformists as well as children of Church of England parents.

In an overt attempt to prevent this, one of St Mary's curates, Herbert Goodenough Rogers, son of the founder of Fullands School, started his own middle class school in 1872 in the building recently vacated by the Taunton College School, now the Municipal Buildings. Opposition to a school open to all shades of Christian opinion came principally from that superbly bigoted philanthropist, Rev F.J. Smith, and from the influential Archdeacon of Taunton, George Anthony Denison. At a public meeting to oppose the Huish proposals Denison almost came to blows with the vicar of St Mary's, Preb W.R. Clark, and incensed the Free Church ministers present. There were further objections to the proposed Huish governing body, claimed to be almost wholly composed of Liberals. By the time that the legal formalities had been completed, Rogers' school was already well established in the only available home for the new Huish boys' school, and in 1875 the two foundations amalgamated under the name of Huish and the leadership of Rogers' headmaster, the Rev Thomas Randell. The setting up of the girls' school was delayed for want of a suitable building and eventually started in 1876 in the former Catholic chapel in the Crescent. Huish's girls' school, however, attracted only two pupils when it first opened, Edward Jeboult's two daughters, Florence and Rosie, aged 8 and 7. Indeed, the poor response proved so embarrassing that the school promptly closed for three months.

Both schools suffered in their rented premises. In 1880 the return of the old College School, from South Road into its former buildings, forced Huish's Boys' School first into the nearby school museum and in 1881 into Green's former Commercial School in East Street. Under Cecil R. Humphrey the school was rebuilt in 1892 on its East Street site and his headmastership was largely responsible for its subsequent success. The girls' school was converted into the Masonic Hall in 1879 and continuous disruption of school life was the inevitable result. It was not until 1891 that the girls moved next door into 20 the Crescent. This was a year after the old College School endowments had been transferred to it, as the Huish Charity proved insufficient to support both schools. It was renamed Bishop Fox's and became Taunton's one and only grammar school for girls. As the two Huish schools drifted apart, there remained a stronger link between them, for Emily M. Reeves, first headmistress of the girls' school, had resigned in 1889 to marry the principal of Bede's College, Durham, none other than the former first headmaster of Huish's Boys' School, Rev Thomas Randell.

Further education also had its place in Jeboult's Taunton. An adult school had been formed in 1815, meeting in St James Street, but it lasted only a short time. A more successful foundation was the Mechanics' Institute, started at the suggestion of Rev T.W. Horsfield of Priory House in 1830. Reading rooms were opened opposite Jacob's Brewery in Mary Street, over 200 members enrolled, and an inaugural lecture on electricity was given at the Theatre by Andrew Crosse of Fyne Court. It attracted gifts of books from, among others, Rev Sydney Smith in 1835, and four years later a new hall was purpose-built by William Beadon of Otterford, on a site in Bath Place given by E.T. Bainbridge, borough MP. The institute moved thence in 1844 and added what was called a Mutual Improvement Class in 1854, but foundered soon after.

More enduring was the School of Science and Art opened in 1856 in connection with departments at Marlborough House, London, with aid from the Privy Council. Science was later dropped and, as the School of Art, it moved into the former Mechanics' Institute hall in Bath Place, where it remained until 1889, when it transferred to the Victoria Rooms on the Parade. Accommodated in new buildings in Corporation Street in 1907, it is a direct ancestor of the present Somerset College of Art and Technology in Wellington Road.

ABOVE LEFT: Taunton College School, 1865, now the Municipal Buildings in Corporation Street, during William Tuckwell's headmastership. Corporation Street was cut through the garden in the foreground in 1894; RIGHT: Taunton College School immediately after its completion in 1870, architect C.E.Giles, builder John Spiller. It became King Alfred's (now King's) College in 1880; BELOW LEFT: Wesleyan College (now Queen's College) in 1860, architect James Wilson of Bath, built by John Mason of Exeter 1846-7; RIGHT: Independent College (Taunton School) fife and drum band outside its first home in Wellington Road, c1865. At the opening of the new school at Fairwater in June 1870 the band headed the procession.

ABOVE: Independent College (Taunton School) on completion, c1870, architect Joseph James of London, builder Henry Davis; LEFT: group of boys at Huish's School, 1888; Edward's sons, Edward and William, are the two on the left; RIGHT: Rev Dr Thomas Randell, first headmaster of Huish's School for Boys from 1874; BELOW: the Crescent looking north, c1865. On the right is the disused Catholic Chapel which from 1875 housed Huish's School for Girls.

ABOVE LEFT: The Convent, South Road, c1865, built as the County Hospital in 1772 but never finished. It became a Convent and Catholic school in 1808; RIGHT: Convent schoolgirls at play, c1865; CENTRE LEFT: Benjamin Ferrey's design for St Mary's Schools, Church Square, built by Henry Davis, Clerk of the Works John Blizard (former schoolmaster there). The foundation stone was laid by the vicar's daughter. Elsie Clark, on 15 September 1866; opened 1867; RIGHT: the dormitory at the Grammar School; BELOW: Public Hall, Bath Place (still standing), built by William Beadon in 1839 and occupied in turn by the Mechanics' Institute and the School of Art, from a drawing by Edward Jeboult.

TIME OFF

For a town of Taunton's size there seldom seems to be any problem in what to do with one's leisure hours. In Jeboult's day, before the advent of the cinema, radio and now television, although the town was less than half its present size, there was much more.

Edward Jeboult's own sporting interests centred on swimming and cricket. The townspeople usually learnt to swim at French Weir, and every few years the magistrates had a troop of young lads before them for nude bathing near the public footpath. It was also the most common venue for accidental drownings or committing suicide; indeed Edward himself had a narrow escape while bathing there as a youth. In 1818 William Savery, a local engineer, had vainly tried for three days and nights to pump the weir pool dry, in an effort to discover why so many had drowned there. The formation of a proper bathing place there was urged in 1856 after a young lad called Silcocks had drowned. Rescue equipment was installed at French Weir and at Tone Bridge, Coal Orchard, Firepool and Obridge, but it was another six years before Jeboult and others succeeded in boarding off an angle of land in French Weir Field called the Bend, prepared the bed of the river, built bathing conveniences and appointed an attendant. Bathers were charged 2d a visit or 2s 6d for a season ticket and plans were also made for a free bathing place at Duckpool.

An annual swimming and diving match was started at the bathing station in 1865. There were relatively few participants, all male, and these apparently competed naked, for a correspondent remarked that 'in future some small article of clothing, if only a Freemason's apron, might with advantage be used by the competitors'. After 1867 the event lapsed, but was revived in 1883 by what became the Taunton Swimming Association, celebrating its centenary this year. The proceedings on this occasion included a 'duck hunt' in which the swimmers chased ducks with clipped wings.

Cricket in the 19th century town was played by a succession of short-lived societies. The first club, formed in 1829 and playing at Orchard Portman, had to be revived in 1846 as a Wednesday team with 40 members. Four years later a Young Men's Cricket Club was started to provide a team of town lads to play the various public schools. Also in 1850 the Vale of Taunton Club was established and received its banner at the first Vivary Park flower show, staged in 1851 by the Taunton Deane Horticultural and Floricultural Society. The Young Men's Club was resuscitated in 1855 as was the Taunton Cricket Club in 1865, playing on the Archery Ground (now the southern section of the Wellington Road Cemetery). In 1873 an existing club based on North Town and the Taunton Vale Club were wound up and a new Taunton Cricket Club rose from their combined ashes.

Edward Jeboult's other sporting passion was bound up with horses and riding. The old Taunton racecourse on Shoreditch (now South) Road, where King's College now stands, was finally abandoned in 1839, and the race committee handed over its surplus funds to East Reach Hospital and also contributed to the cost of a new east window for St Mary's. Taunton races were restarted at Trull Moor in 1846 and again briefly revived on the 18th century course near Blackbrook in 1886, where the Taunton Vale Foxhounds and the Taunton Harriers also staged their steeplechases for several years. From racing, the Taunton gentlemen turned to fishing, but in Jeboult's youth the Tone was severely polluted: above the town by a whole succession of cloth and silk mills. Below the bridge were others plus the added bonus of the town's sewage, which accumulated at the weirs, particularly at Firepool, Obridge and Bathpool.

An attempt to restore salmon to the river began in June 1868 when the Tone Fishery Association was formed at Scarlett's Nag's Head Hotel. The services of Frank Buckland, the David Bellamy of his day and one of HM Inspectors of salmon fisheries, were engaged and the following winter he sent 1,500 salmon eggs to be hatched in troughs at the museum in the New Market, and the young fish were turned into the river in the summer of 1869. The odd salmon was occasionally seen in the Tone but further grayling ova had to be introduced in 1874. Two years later it was agreed hopeless to try to make the Tone a salmon river, although the Fishery Association was revived in 1879 to prevent illegal netting and establish rules for angling.

In the days before Taunton's expansion the cheapest recreation for the townsfolk was a simple walk by the river, upstream to Bishops Hull or down to Bathpool. Edward Jeboult's father was always proud of having been a prime mover in laying out Priory Walk, across the fields where St Augustine and Winchester streets now run. Further downstream through the Creechbarrow estate ran what was, until the 18th century, part of the main road to Bridgwater, known mistakenly to the locals as Roman Road. After the present main route by way of Halcon Corner was developed, the old way became a picturesque overgrown lane. The owner of Creechbarrow House (now the Creech Castle Hotel), Capt George Beadon, tried to have it closed as a public right of way and, when legal methods failed, he erected fences and locked gates across the path. Popular feelings ran high, and in 1870 a well organised crowd from the town, determined to assert their rights, tore down the obstructions. Beadon claimed that he had been assaulted by 'a drunken thieving rabble', although in court the magistrates dismissed his charges. To keep the lane open and other of their favourite haunts the ramblers devised one of those typically Victorian groups, the Taunton Association for the Protection of Public Footpaths and Rights of Way, electing as its first secretary none other than Edward Jeboult. The old Roman Road is now submerged beneath a sea of red brick but its misleading name lives on.

For a night out in Edward's youth the popular resort was the theatre built by Henry Lee at Silver Street in 1800. In 1835 Henry's son, Herbert Lee, sold his entire circuit of theatres to Edward Deane Davis, formerly of the Plymouth and Southampton boards, who employed William Stansell to redecorate the Taunton building. The old classical drop scene by C.W. Bampfylde of Hestercombe gave way to a new one by Channing of Brighton Theatre Royal. At only 37 ft wide, 80 ft deep and 24 ft high the structure was tiny by modern standards, but it was fully equipped with panelled boxes, pit and gallery. With a company of nine men and six women Davis recreated the delights of pieces such as *The Haunted Moor or the Prophet of the Druid's Stone*, eked out with a farce, songs like *When thy bosom heaves a sigh* or a hornpipe from Little Master Davis, the manager's son.

Unfortunately, houses were poor. On one evening in 1837 the takings did not even pay for the gas; on another less than a dozen tickets were sold, and for *Virginius and the Illustrious Stranger*, the manager's benefit night, 'the curtain rose to 17s and fell to £3'. In desperation Davis engaged West's equestrian spectacular which restaged the battle of Waterloo, *Mazeppa* and *Turpin's Ride to York or the Death of Black Bess*. Even then receipts were low, the behaviour of young roughs in the audience brought out the police to keep order and harsh winters kept others away. In 1838 a jug thrown from the gallery injured a tradesman's wife in the pit and, to counter such adverse publicity, the celebrated actress Harriett Waylett was engaged on two occasions. In 1839 Edmund Kean's son, Charles, proved an even greater draw and the theatre was again redecorated. The new proscenium arch bore the figure of Shakespeare flanked by the emblems of comedy and tragedy and garlanded with musical instruments, while the boxes were topped with a cornice of busts and subjects from the ruins of Pompeii. In the course of the summer season of some 12 weeks over 100 different pieces were played, but Davis still lost several hundred pounds. In September famous singers Emma Romer and John Templeton double-booked at Bristol and Taunton and chose to disappoint Davis.

It became clear that Taunton would only turn out in strength for household names and these Davis tried to provide: Wallack, Balfe, the Destin family and Kean again. But in 1841 the *Taunton Courier* could still speak of 'deserted benches night after night' and 'the indifference of our population to the claims of the manager'. In 1842 the evils of the theatre were denounced from St James's pulpit and the following year the fatal blow fell. Davis's theatre at Bridport burnt to the ground with the loss of most of his costumes and scenery. The Taunton theatre was sold to Mr Holmes, who rechristened it the Theatre Royal without any obvious justification for the title. A single season was enough to convince Holmes that he had little chance of making a success of the venture. The last recorded performance was in July 1844 when Capt Harvey Tuckett, formerly of Lord Cardigan's 11th Hussars, appeared as Falstaff. By October the theatre had been sold to builder William Pettit, who demolished it in 1846 to redevelop the east side of Silver Street. Today its approximate site is prosaicly occupied by a betting shop.

In default of a theatre Tauntonians turned to the old Parade Assembly Rooms in the Market House, although these were more suited to concerts and bazaars. The gap was bridged by the building of new Assembly Rooms by Thomas George Meetens behind his London (now County) Hotel, which opened with a ball given by the West Somerset Yeomanry Cavalry in 1849. It was decorated with classic groups of figures, including those of the Queen, Prince Albert and the Duke of Wellington, lit by gas and heated by two large fireplaces. There in 1852 John Browne, an escaped American negro slave, spoke on the horrors of slavery. The Rooms proved so popular that in 1861 they were rebuilt, forming a main auditorium 100 ft long, 40 ft wide and 30 ft high. Meetens arranged a grand County ball to reopen the building, but the death of Prince Albert only three days before caused its cancellation. News of the Prince's death came in the form of a telegram carried into the morning service at St Mary's while the choir was singing *Happy Soul, thy days are ended* to a tune which Albert himself had composed.

In the first year after their building, the new Assembly Rooms attracted Charles Kean, Jenny Lind, Sims Reeves, Charles Matthews, the original Christy minstrels and the Lyric Opera Company with *Il Trovatore*. It was here that all major balls and dinners were held, and where a roller skating rink was installed for several months from 1875 (for that proved a craze as short lived as skateboarding). Charles (later Sir Charles) Hallé performed there three times, in 1869, 1875 and 1878. Within its walls in 1873 Howard Paul delivered 'a quaint song on Darwin's pet theory' with a gorilla that danced the Polka, and in 1882 Edith O'Gorman, the escaped num, gave 'a startling and thrilling lecture'. It sheltered African explorer and journalist H.M. Stanley, when he spoke to packed houses in 1878 and 1886, the D'Oyly Carte Opera Company on the first of many visits with *HMS Pinafore* in 1880, and Dr Barnardo, who spoke in the same month on his London homes for destitute children. London pantomimes came regularly, one in 1882 under the incredible title: *Little Bo Peep who lost her sheep or Harlequin Boy Blue, Princess Superba, Goldenheart the Good and Alcohol the Wicked Demon of the Universe*. For the rest of the century and beyond, the London Hotel Assembly Rooms (now the County Ballroom) provided the major social, dramatic and musical centre for the town.

To provide an even larger meeting place for the town, Edward Jeboult was commissioned in 1863 to convert and adapt the Assize Hall in Taunton Castle. The great room was refloored, a new window inserted, waiting, dressing and refreshment areas provided and a large gallery inserted at the west end. It was boasted that 350 could dine there, and that it could accommodate 700 sitting and 1,400 standing (mainly for political or great religious meetings). There in 1864 Jeboult's father-in-law, Samuel Summerhayes, staged his first series of weekly 'People's Concerts', featuring his celebrated pianist daughter, Cecilia, who had made her London debut at Manchester Square six years before. Events such as an industrial exhibition by the Taunton Working Men's Association were held there in 1869, and Frederick Neebe's Exeter pantomime of *Dick Whittington* proved so successful in 1872 that the company remained for a full month. Threats to demolish the Castle for redevelopment led the Somerset Archaeological and Natural History Society to step in and buy the building in 1874. After their museum was moved thence from the New Market in Fore Street, the old Assize Hall was less readily available for public performances and meetings. Indeed the purchase was only made possible by a succession of annual fancy dress balls at the London Hotel Assembly Rooms, formerly the rival establishment.

The inns and hotels of the town functioned as the principal social centres, many with their own bowling and outings clubs and friendly societies. What is now the Castle Hotel on Castle Green was built by the Easton family in about 1815 as a private two-storey house, visually to balance the Winchester Arms. The addition of two further storeys in the 20th century has, however, destroyed that concept. Mary Sweet, whose father William had taken over the Castle Inn in North Street in 1786 and whose mother, Martha, had gone bankrupt in running it in 1815, converted the house into Sweet's Hotel and opened it in 1834. Unwise speculation in the carriage trade led in turn to Mary's bankruptcy and she was followed by James Fackrell from the Squirrel Inn at Wellington. Robert Giles succeeded him in 1844 and in 1850, the year of his death, opened the town's first billiard hall on Castle Green, now converted into hotel garages. Giles's widow, Elizabeth, struggled on for three years before the hotel passed to Charlotte Clarke, its former barmaid. During her tenure the Tap, now the Stagecoach Inn, and the stables behind it burnt to the ground in 1863. Charlotte died at her former hotel in 1876, although it had already been taken over by Sydney Hitchcock. Hitchcock's successor, George Rawle, was a well-known racehorse owner who died in harness at the hotel in 1888. During Rawles' tenure plans were laid to combine Clarke's Hotel and what had become the Castle Hotel in North Street. A limited company was floated in 1887 with a share capital of £20,000, but disagreements with the proprietor of the Castle Hotel, John Withycombe, put paid to the project. The union of the two hotels had to wait until 1927.

The pre-eminence of the London Hotel in East Street has already been demonstrated. To his lucrative Assembly Rooms Meetens added the West Somerset Club in 1863, involving the conversion of three ground-floor rooms for reading and billiards. The hotel, with 31 bedrooms, 21 dining, sitting and other rooms, was sold in 1887 for £6,000 to H.H. Gill of the Railway Hotel. The latter building, to the south of the Station and now converted into offices, had developed a worthy reputation under its first proprietor, Charles Waghorn. Gill had married the widow of the former owner, Edwin Douch, who had risen from being landlord of the Royal Marine Inn and died in 1875. In due course both the London and Railway Hotels were taken over by Mrs Gill's nephew, George Saunders.

One hotel with a less than savoury reputation was the White Hart on the corner of Fore and High Streets, saddled with hazy traditions of Monmouth bloodshed in the 17th century. In the early 1840s it was kept by Frederick George Manning, son of the landlord of the Bear Inn in North Street, and his wife Maria. In 1849, having moved to London, husband and wife were jointly convicted of the murder of an Irishman, and hanged together before a crowd of 50,000. Theirs being considered one of the crimes of the century, the Mannings' effigies long adorned the Chamber of Horrors at Madame Tussauds. The inn proved no more fortunate for a subsequent proprietor, Thomas Wood, who died in 1861 after a riding accident in the stable archway. It was converted into a general store in 1864-5 by Meyer Jacobs under the sign of 'the Little Dustpan' and later became the Devon and Somerset Stores.

Taunton also knew how to celebrate the grand occasions. The nine-year old Edward Jeboult could well remember Queen Victoria's coronation day in 1838, when the town's celebrations began at 5 am with the ringing of church bells and the firing of pistols and a cannon. A lengthy trades procession moved slowly through the streets from Barrack Field and a lunch (for men only!) was served on the Parade. Together they consumed 2,200 lbs of meat, 1,000 lbs of plum pudding, 4,000 quarts of ale, 2,060 loaves and 1,000 oz of tobacco smoked in 2,000 clay pipes. A tea for 2,700 children followed in the afternoon when the youngsters managed to down 3½ hogsheads of that luxury beverage, coffee. There was a firework display in the evening and a public dance was led off by Joseph Anderson, a wealthy tradesman, partnering 'Fisher Sal' Courtney, an old Taunton character. Four years later the Great West Pennard cheese, weighing 9¼ cwt, which had been made from the milk of 737 cows and presented to the new Queen, was exhibited at the Parade Assembly Rooms. It was later cut and found to be inedible, which rather spoilt the object of the exercise.

The arrival of the railway meant that many Tauntonians could witness national occasions for themselves. In 1858 the GWR ran excursion trains from Taunton for the marriage of the Princess Royal and Prince Frederick William of Prussia. The town's Crimean cannon was carted into French Weir and a rather protracted 21-gun salute was fired. The town also knew how to welcome heroes. In 1863 Capt J.H. Speke, discoverer of the source of the Nile, was greeted at the Station by the band of the West Somerset Yeomanry Cavalry and taken amid cheering crowds to Shire Hall to receive a congratulatory address. The following month he was honoured with a dinner and ball in the Grand Jury Room at Shire Hall and, in 1864, the Lord Lieutenant presented him with a pair of Egyptian vases in the Nisi Prius Court. A similarly warm welcome was given to Major John Chard, the hero of the battle of Rorke's Drift, on his return to his native Somerset in 1879.

There were of course innumerable annual occasions when Taunton turned out in force to enjoy itself: the Assize fairs on Castle Green, until the Market trustees banned them in 1871, the regular visits by circuses such as Wombwell's Royal Menagerie and Sanger's Zoological and Equestrian Hippodrome (1858), and the November the Fifth fireworks and blazing tar barrels, similarly exiled by the Market Trustees in 1890. The November jollifications took an uglier turn in 1850 when it was learned that the Pope had verbally abused Queen Victoria. Anti-papal sermons were preached in the town's churches and the effigies of Pius IX and Cardinal Wiseman were processed onto Castle Green, hanged from a large gallows and burned on a massive bonfire while the fireworks exploded around them.

LEFT: Drawing by Edward Jeboult of the original bathing station he helped to establish at French Weir in 1862; RIGHT: footbridge over French Weir, c1865.

MR. COMER

Has the honor to announce that his

SIXTH AND LAST

SUBSCRIPTION CONCERT

For the Season, will take place

AT HIS ROOMS, NO. 6, CRESCENT,

On **WEDNESDAY EVENING,** the 29th of **APRIL, 1846,**

To commence at Half-past Seven o'clock.

FIRST PART.

OVERTURE, "Il flauto magico" ... ... MOZART.

GLEE, Mrs. MILLAR, Mr. MILLAR, Mr. LING, and Mr.
    COMER, "Give me the Harp" ... ... Sir J. STEVENSON.

SONG, Mr. COMER, Di guegl' occhi ... ... RICCI.

TRIO, Mrs. MILLAR, Mr. MILLAR, and Mr. COMER,
    "Turn on old time" from "Maritana" ... ... WALLACE.

ARIA, Mrs. MILLAR, "Sommo Cielo" ... ... PACCINI.

TRIO, Piano-forte, Violin, Violoncello, Miss WINGROVE,
    Mr. S. SUMMERHAYES, and Mr. COMER. ... ...

SONG, Mr. MILLAR, "Our home is on the sea, boy"... ... MILLAR.

DUETTO, Mr. MILLAR and Mr. COMER, "AH idea" ... ROSSINI.

GLEE, Mrs. MILLAR, Mr. MILLAR, Mr. LING, and Mr.
    COMER, "The merriest time" ... ... ALDRIDGE.

SECOND PART.

SONG, Mr. COMER, "Friend of the brave" ... ... Dr. CALCOTT

TRIO, Mrs. MILLAR, Mr. MILLAR, and Mr. COMER, "La
    mia Dorabella" ... ... MOZART.

BALLAD, Mr. MILLAR, "Believe me if all those endearing
    young charms" ... ...

FANTASIA, Piano-forte, Miss WINGROVE, "La Rose"
    (By particular desire.)

SONG, Mrs. MILLAR, "The blind flower Girl" ... ... MILLAR.

SOLO and CHORUS, "Now tramp" ... ... Sir H. R. BISHOP.

FINALE, "God save the Queen" ... ...

Miss WINGROVE will preside at the Piano-forte.

LEFT: Programme for concert given by John Comer at 6 The Crescent in 1846, including Samuel Summerhayes; ABOVE: Thomas George Meetens's London Hotel, c1865. He was succeeded by Samuel C. Tyack in 1870; CENTRE: White Hart Hotel on the corner of High and Fore streets, 1863, held by J. Higgins Hanny. By 1866 he had moved the inn sign to East Reach; BELOW: the former White Hart in 1865, immediately after its conversion by Meyer Jacobs; later the Devon and Somerset Stores.

ABOVE LEFT: Bazaar in the vestibule of Shire Hall, c1865. Note the orchestra in the balcony; RIGHT: Clarke's Giles's Family Hotel, c1865, now the Castle Hotel. The small coach is probably the hotel horse 'bus which ferried guests to and from the Station; BELOW LEFT: Phoenix Inn, East Street, c1865, held since 1855 by John Gill. The shop on the right was occupied by William Morley, photographer and frame maker; RIGHT: Castle Hotel, North Street, kept by William Pattison, c1865; CENTRE: Castle Bow, part of Clarke's Hotel, with Corn Exchange on the left. Sign to the left of the bow reads 'To the Baths' which were set up in the Castle by James Dyer in 1851 but had closed again by 1854; BELOW: gymnasium in Bridge Street opened by Monsieur Bourrecoud from the Gymnase Cantonal, Lausanne, in 1861.

VALE OF TAUNTON DEANE HORTICULTURAL AND FLORICULTURAL SOCIETY.

The annual meeting of the subscribers to this society was held on Wednesday at the Market House, Mr. C. BALLANCE in the chair.

Mr. Kingsbury, the Secretary, read the following report from the committee : —

"Your committee have now the satisfaction of submitting the annual report of the society, and, notwithstanding the heavy expenditure of last year, it is satisfactory for them to state that there is now a sum of £35. 9s. 2d., in the hands of the Treasurer, as shown by the annual balance sheet, now produced, and which remains in the hands of the Secretary for inspection by the subscribers. Your committee recommend the propriety of holding two exhibitions during the present year, and that prizes in accordance with the list now produced should be offered for amateurs; and your committee would recommend that the present meeting should authorize the committee to award such prizes for nurserymen as would increase the attractions of the show. Your committee would further recommend that a poultry exhibition should be held in connection with the society at the June show, and that a sum not exceeding £10 should be awarded in prizes, and that the show should be held and kept open for two days, namely on Wednesday and Thursday, the 21st and 22nd days of June, and that the second Horticultural Exhibition be held on the 6th of September."

Having read this, Mr. Kingsbury remarked that some alterations had been made in the list of prizes, some having been awarded last year for things which were not in season.

A discussion took place upon the part of the report referring to the Poultry Exhibition, but it was ultimately resolved that the details referred to should be left to the committee.

Mr. HORSEY said he had received a letter from Mr. Marshall containing the suggestion that provision should be made for the protection of the poultry in their coops. This matter was also left to the committee.

On the motion of Mr. HORSEY, seconded by Mr GREEN, it was unanimously resolved that the report now read be adopted, as also the schedule of prizes produced by the Secretary.

Mr. HORSEY moved, Dr. BURRIDGE seconded, and it was unanimously resolved, that Henry Badcock, Esq., be appointed President of the Society for the ensuing year. J. F. Norman, Esq., was elected Treasurer, and Mr. Kingsbury was re-appointed Hon. Secretary, thanks being given him for his past exertions.

A vote of thanks having been awarded to the chairman the meeting separated.

ABOVE LEFT: George Hotel, High Street, c1865; RIGHT: east side of North Street, 1860, showing James Scarlett's Nag's Head Inn; CENTRE ABOVE: Sugar Loaf Inn, Park Street, c1865, demolished 1885 for rebuilding of St Saviour's Home for Boys; CENTRE BELOW: Parade by West Somerset Yeomanry in North Street, c1865; BELOW: parade on the Parade, c1865; RIGHT: the Vale of Taunton Deane Horticultural and Floricultural Society, 1854.

ABOVE: The horse 'bus to the rescue in Bridge Street during the great floods, of 1889. In the distance is the George Inn, North Town, now the site of the Classic Cinema; LEFT: Taunton Barracks as drawn by Edward Jeboult; RIGHT: the Tone 'above the sewage works'.

ABOVE: Family group, 1879: standing — Frank, Harold, Edward
Jeboult, Rose, Charles, Herbert; seated — Florence, Edward, Hettie
Jeboult (nursing Reginald), William; LEFT: Edward Jeboult's two eldest
sons, Charles Henry (born 1864) and Herbert Edward Summerhayes
(born 1863), taken in 1882; RIGHT: Edward's eldest daughter, Florence
(1867-1917).

ANOTHER GENERATION

The name Jeboult has gone from Taunton. Considering that Edward and Hettie, in addition to their three daughters, managed to produce a grand total of nine sons this is somewhat surprising, although it reflects the excitement which travel seems to have held for the next generation.

The eldest son Herbert (Bertie), born in 1863, served as a chorister at St James's and then went for about a year to the offices of the *Taunton Courier* and *Somerset County Herald* on the Parade. He also worked in the china shop run by his cousin Frederick J. Jeboult at Cheapside, and then with his father at Station Road. A great sportsman, his health was endangered at the age of 17 by 'over-activity', whereupon his father persuaded him to learn the 'cello. He seems to have developed a wanderlust, aggravated by the exploits of the second son, his brother Charlie. Edward had sent Charlie to work in the offices of Pinchards', the Paul Street solicitors, but he was unable to settle there. Eventually and after much persuasion, Edward reluctantly apprenticed him in 1879 at the age of 15 to George Sully, a Bridgwater ship broker, and Charlie began a succession of adventurous voyages that took him around the world. One ship sank after a collision, leaving him afloat in an open boat; on another occasion he was washed overboard and it was a minor miracle that he ever survived. He settled briefly in Sydney, Australia, and it was his influence which tempted Bertie and the third son, Frank, to join him. Charles returned to England to marry a West Monkton girl in 1890, but died near Minehead only six years later, at the age of only 32. Bertie remained in Australia, where his 'cello playing, a rare accomplishment in the Antipodes, stood him in good stead. He toured New Zealand and played at the Melbourne Exhibition under Cowen of London.

In 1879 Edward had apprenticed Frank, then aged 13, to Charles Lewis, grocer, tea dealer and wine merchant at what is now the Tudor Tavern in Fore Street. Frank was no more settled than Charlie, and a year later he was out in Calcutta, and in 1883 set up house in Sydney permanently. Ernest and Arthur, the fourth and seventh sons, both died as babies before their first birthday, but the sixth son Reginald also emigrated.

Reggie, born in 1872, had been a chorister at Holy Trinity and St John's, joined the bicycle corps of the 13th Prince Albert's Somerset Militia and, like Bertie, learned the 'cello. He worked for a time at William Crockett's photographic studio in East Street and was eventually apprenticed to Sale and Spiller, Bridge Street, for four years. He finally went in 1891 to Newton's Rowbarton works to train as an electrical engineer, and in 1897 moved to London, having secured a patent for a new type of electric light fitting. For a time he had his younger brother Edward (Ted) as a partner, but subsequently he emigrated to Canada, where he died in 1932.

The eighth brother William, born in 1876, was a member of St John's choir and went to the School of Art in Bath Place. In 1891 he was despatched to Easton and Waldegrave's Whitehall Iron Works and, as an engineer, eventually took his talents to Birmingham. Ted, the ninth and youngest, born in 1878, was trained up with his father but, following old Edward Jeboult's death, the Station Road works were closed and Ted was apprenticed to a North Street ironmonger. Later he became a manager for Nicholls & Co, the Taunton sports and 'cycle agents and, after his brief London partnership with Reggie, moved to Birmingham as one of the first managers for the Halford Cycle Co, opening and managing shops there and at Sheffield, Bristol, Nottingham, Derby, Bristol, Manchester and London.

Neither of the two surviving girls married. Florence became a governess and then a kindergarten teacher under Madame Meynier at the Alexandra College (now Wilton Lodge). Eventually she trained as a nurse at the East Reach hospital and worked for several years in London. During the First World War she was sent by the Red Cross to an English hospital in France. While there she became seriously ill and returned to England, dying in 1917, three days short of her fiftieth birthday. Her sister Rosie managed Clement Smith's music shop in East Street, living at home with her mother at 1 Belvedere Road until her premature death in 1901, aged only 32.

To Tauntonians of the present, however, the only Jeboult who is still generally remembered is Harold, fifth son of Edward and Hettie, born in 1871. He was naturally musical from an early age, sang in St James's choir under John Wood and obtained a music scholarship to St John's, Harlow in Essex, at the age of 13. He studied under J. Warriner at Dunster and also went to the Independent College (Taunton School) for a short time. Unfortunately his health was never good and the doctor ordered his withdrawal from formal education. To the rescue came his cousin, W.G. Rawlinson, who paid for his tuition in organ and piano with T.J. Dudeney, under whom he served as assistant organist at St James's, St John's and Holy Trinity. He tried his hand at composition, producing several rousing marches, and in 1888 became organist at Holy Trinity, and choir master there three years later. In 1894 he became a fellow of the Royal College of Organists, bought out Dudeney's musical practice and moved with his family into Belvedere Road. The final accolade came in 1897, when organist Alfred P. Standley moved to Rossall School and Harold was elevated to the organ stool of St Mary's, a post he was to hold for the rest of his life.

He carried his composing a stage further when he wrote the score for a local opera, *In the Days of the Siege* (with libretto by county cricketer, G.B. Nicholls), based on Taunton's Civil War experiences under Robert Blake. It was presented for three nights at the London Hotel Assembly Rooms in April 1898 under the baton of F.J. Moore. Harry Frier, the well-known local artist, executed the scenery and the cast included such prominent local names as Charles Goodland, Theo Taylor, F.C. Goodman and G.B. Nicholls himself. On the first night Taunton's MP, Col Welby, had to drive his own coach home, having emerged from the performance to find his coachman dead drunk in the back. The proceeds were divided between the County Cricket Club and the Town Band. The opera was revived in January 1900 in aid of the local fund for South African War Reservists and led to the foundation of the Taunton Amateur Operatic Society. The same duo, Jeboult and Nicholls, wrote the new society's second opera, *Peerless and Peerlot*, presented in 1901. Harold also served as conductor to the Taunton Madrigal Society from 1904 until the First World War, and his organ recitals after evensong at St Mary's were extremely popular.

Harold also played his part in perpetuating a delightful family story with links back to the early Jeboults in Salisbury. In 1898 there appeared in the *Pall Mall Magazine* extracts from a collection of letters and papers all dated 1810-12. They concerned a certain John Highmore Jeboult of Salisbury, whose father, John Reginald, had been brother to William Jeboult, who in turn had ended his days at Taunton in 1817. The papers had been discovered in the secret compartment of a large brass-bound desk in the possession of the Preston family of Smithfield, Virginia. The desk had been taken as the spoils of battle by Col James Patton Preston in Canada during the war of 1812, and the hidden drawer was not discovered until over 80 years later.

The papers showed that John Highmore Jeboult had enlisted in the 1st Somerset Militia in 1810 and the following year volunteered to join the 41st Regiment. He had also fallen in love with Elenora Millicent Hayter, and in the desk was found a lock of her golden hair wrapped in a protective verse, which urged Heaven to 'protect you whilst you're on the seas, secure from murdering foes and stormy breeze'. The couple's courtship apparently had not been wholly plain sailing. A rift developed after she acused him of ignoring her in the street, and his suit was not helped when his character was vilified by a brother officer. It was two years before their quarrel was mended and their betrothal renewed. By that time Jeboult found himself facing the enemy as a Lieutenant in Quebec. In the same month that he and Elenora were reconciled, September 1812, his commanding officer, Major G.G. Friend, wrote to Jeboult's father that his son had been killed in the act of valiantly saving the Regimental colours. The Major had been entrusted with the young Lieutenant's effects and he wrote that he was placing his sad letter in the secret compartment of the desk, which he would return to England. The changing fortunes of war ensured that the desk and its contents never reached their destination.

Harold was delighted. Here was a member of his own family who had not only been an officer and a gentleman but had died bravely in the service of his country. As John Highmore Jeboult had briefly served in the Somerset Militia, Harold saw this as sufficient justification for placing a tablet in St Mary's church to record the tragic but memorable event. It was duly unveiled by the Mayor of Taunton in April 1914.

Later that same year Harold tried to obtain possession of the original papers from Canada and surprisingly succeeded. With them came further information that was not quite so welcome. The magazine article had evidently prompted considerable correspondence, and the Preston family had heard, among others, from the daughter of John Highmore, the Countess Beaumont of Paris. It then became clear that the young officer had not died on the battlefield after all, but had recovered from his wounds. He had returned to England, spurned Elenora Hayter, married a second lady and raised a family. References in old Edward's family scrapbook indicated that he was probably the Captain Jeboult who used to visit his uncle, William Jeboult, in Taunton until he made disparaging remarks about William's new house at Wilton, after which he was not invited again. Thus to this day the tablet graces the south aisle of St Mary's, commemorating a valiant end which never occurred.

Harold lived on at Belvedere Road with Hettie, his mother, as the family gradually drifted away from Taunton to the four corners of the globe. Mother and son later moved to Birch Grove, where Edward's widow finally died on 8 April 1924 at the grand age of 81. Harold had never been a robust man and his health gave way not long after his mother's death. He died just over a year later on 16 July 1925, aged 54, and, in accordance with his last wishes, was dressed in the cassock and surplice which he had worn so often at St Mary's. Of that large family which Edward had sired there were only two, William from Birmingham and Ted from London, who came to see Harold off on his final journey. The last Taunton Jeboult had passed to his rest.

Athletics prize won by Edward's son Herbert when aged 17.

Taunton Athletic Sports,

THURSDAY, JULY 15, 1880.

SECOND PRIZE
220 YARDS FLAT RACE

Presented by *Taunton Athletic Society.*

ABOVE LEFT: Herbert (born 1863) as a young man; CENTRE: Charles Henry (born 1864); RIGHT: Frank (born 1865), reluctantly posed; BELOW LEFT: Harold (born 1871), with the text for the day, and in musical mood; CENTRE: Edward Jeboult's second daughter, Rosie, born 1868; RIGHT: the elegant Reginald Callaway Jeboult (born 1872).

6th of July.

Dear Mater & Pater.

It is nothing but Rain rain, rain. But Ted & I are quite dry as we stay in a shed out behind the house & make rafts torpeadoes etc.

We are making a torpeado about [illegible] to a windmill for

Mrs Bailey to keep the Birds from the fruit. I hope pater is better & you all right

Iremainx Yourlovingso

[illegible]

We went out fishing yesterday, but we didn't catch anything because we took the wrong bait, so we set a night-line

hook instead. We We are having prosper times here, in the old sheds. And how is old dad. Give my love to Bessie and all at home

Yours Tarley
T.E.D

How is New, Ben, Teyer Buronice, Owl &c.

ABOVE: 'Tod' (William Alexander, born 1876) writes to his parents, and brother Edward Taunton chips in, somewhat irreverently; LEFT: William Alexander as a boy; RIGHT: Edward Taunton Jeboult (standing back left, born 1878) and friends, c1890.

91

Of Edward and Hettie Jeboult's twelve children, five died in infancy;
Edward Jeboult recorded their passing, on this poignant page of his family
history.

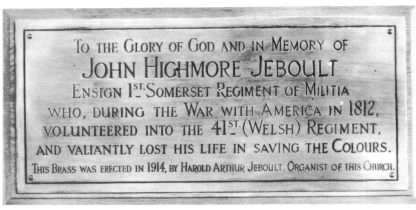

LETTER No. 14.

QUEBEC, *Sept. 24th,* 1812.

MR. REGINALD JEBOULT,

ESTEEMED SIR :—

It is with a feeling of profound sorrow that I seat myself to perform the heavy office of a bearer of evil tidings. You will surmise, that I have news, and not good news, of your absent son. Mr. Jeboult has gone through every engagement, with distinguished bravery; his captaincy was an assured thing. On Thursday evening, towards the close of the engagement, Mr. Jeboult saw the color-bearer over-borne, and in the space of one moment, as it seemed, he made a gallant rush, captured the colors, and carried them possibly one hundred yards, when his arm being wounded, and the flag drooping, his foot caught and he fell, carrying the colors with him. We thought him not seriously wounded at first, but a short time soon evidenced there was some deep wound yet unknown, and the surgeon on examining him, advised that he be not removed as long as life remained. I got to him as quickly as could be, and found him entirely conscious, and perfectly calm. He pressed my hand and made several efforts to speak, but could not. Just before the end he said quite clearly, " Tell Elenora," tried to say more but failed, smiled faintly and then died, with that same loveable light of joyous manliness upon his countenance as he had borne in life. Your son has left a noble legacy, in the name he bears in his regiment for bravery, generosity, gentleness and truth. He had completely lived down that vile Martin slander, and no greater proof of his worth could be given, than the large-hearted generosity with which he endeavored to rescue Martin from the ignominy he so richly deserved. Your son charged me with the care of his effects, including a desk in which the papers are concealed in a secret drawer, of which he tells me you know the working. It is my present purpose to send this by post, but in the event of any further trouble, I will place it in the compartment named, trusting they may one day come safely to hand.

I don't presume to offer consolation to a family smitten beneath so crushing a blow. Simply testifying to his worth, to my sorrow for you, my sympathy with you, I beg to subscribe myself,

Yr. obliged humble serv't.,

G. G. FRIEND,

ABOVE: Tablet in south aisle of St Mary's commemorating a valiant death that never, in fact, occurred; BELOW: the letter in the *Pall Mall Magazine* of July 1898 that prompted Harold Jeboult to commemorate the 'event'.

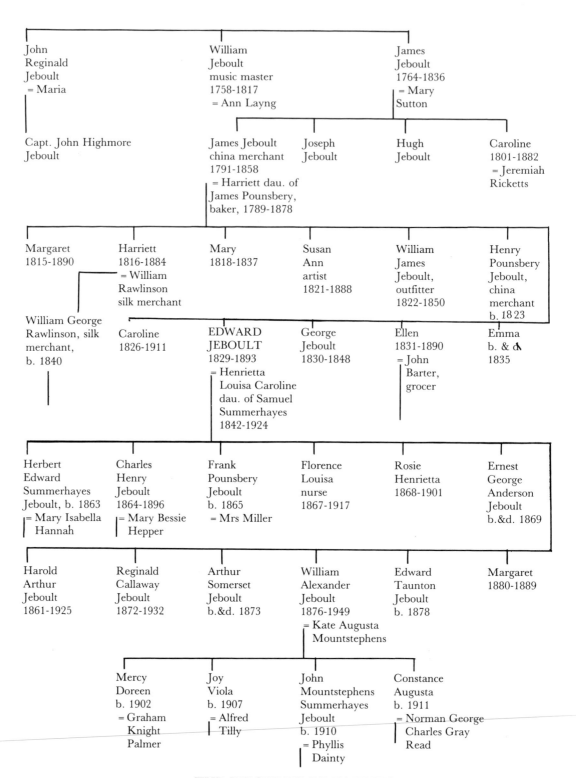

THE JEBOULTS OF TAUNTON

JEBOULT'S LEGACY

Apart from a handful of illustrations, such as the maps which decorate the endpapers and virtually span Edward Jeboult's Taunton, cuttings from a contemporary copy of the *Somerset County Gazette,* and some additional portraits, all the material in this book has been carefully reproduced from Edward Jeboult's two massive albums — his History of the Town of Taunton, and his In Memoriam Jeboult Family, and from the later family scrapbook. To ensure the best possible reproduction and to remain faithful to the originals, the vast majority of the illustrations have been reproduced to the same size as they appear in those books, or nearly so. Many of the pictures are quite small.

The first book runs to 165 folios, and the second to 333 folios, with many further manuscript and printed items interleaved. To convey some of the atmosphere of those remarkable volumes, a selection of facsimile pages and entries follow, together with the remaining portraits of the less relevant members of the family, not included in previous chapters.

Editor

Jeboult's Taunton — the original first volume.

The title page of Edward's *History of the Town of Taunton.*

History of the past.

But taking all into consideration, great and important changes took place in this town. We must not forget the establishment of Banks, the development of the Post Office, the improvement of the Tone Navigation, and last, but not least, the formation of the first Sunday or Poor Man's School. Next week we propose to treat of Taunton during the 19th century, in which it appears to us that far greater improvements have taken place than in any previous age.

TAUNTON DURING THE PRESENT CENTURY.

In attempting to describe Taunton of the existing time, we do not propose to treat of the various streets, buildings, &c., as this would be far too much for one short paper, but we would endeavour to point out the distinctive character and features which mark the present from the past ages of its existence, and show the advance which has taken place in its various institutions and local arrangements.

1st, Ecclesiastically. At the commencement of this century, Taunton was, (like the country generally) at a very low ebb, in all religious or ecclesiastical matters. Probably the effects of the continental wars and the revolutionary and infidel state of France, together with great apathy in religious matters among the higher classes, greatly contributed to render the people careless. Gothic architecture suffered from the same cause, and these times produced many of those barbarous designs and pagan ideas exemplified in some of our modern church alterations and "Salem," "Ebenezer," and "Bethel" chapels. But towards the year 1840 things began to change. The clergy and ministers stirred up their flocks, and from that time to the

present the Church of England, together with all the various dissenting denominations and Roman Catholics, seem to vie in excelling each other in these good works, and such church and chapel buildings and restorations were never before witnessed. We should say that there must be at least double the church and and chapel accommodation and four times as many services as formerly, so that if the inhabitants do not attain a higher degree of morality and religion it is not from the want of opportunity. Taunton also boasts of many and good branches of home and foreign missionary work.

2nd, Socially. The homes of the people have certainly greatly improved with the times. The higher classes now live in great comfort in their suburban villas, the middle in better and healthier houses, and the working people are generally removed out of the close and dark alleys or colleges to more open and pleasant neighbourhoods. The

[F. CLARKE, TYP., TAUNTON.

A facsimile page (23) from Jeboult's book.

Notice to members of the Jeboult family

This Book was prepared - arranged & made
by Edward Jeboult 3rd Son of James and
Harriet Jeboult of Taunton. Co Somerset
from papers - data - information pictures &c
collected for many years by Ed Jeboult
The Book is intended to be held by the
following Representatives of the family
1st. Those residing in Taunton - (the Senior)
2nd   "   "   "   England   "
3rd   "   "   "   Elsewhere   "

It is hoped. that Some member of the family
will take sufficient interest in the Subject
to enter up the various events as they occur
So that it may be handed down to posterity
in a somewhat Complete form

                    Edward Jeboult
                    July 1890

Edward Jeboult's exhortation to his family at the front of his family album.

Particulars of the "Jeboult" family

In the years 1880-7 Edward Jeboult of 13 Station road, Taunton Commenced enquiries as to the early history of this family — & he Continued investigating for about five seven years during which time he had various Communications with persons of numerous towns & Countries, and caused investigations to be made at the Record office in London, at the office of Somerset Herald, and of many other parties likely to be possessed of informa tion as to family history. His Success was not great, and he is of opinion that the family-name must have undergone alteration, as many others have done — All parties seem to agree that the name was either French or derived from the French, and may have been De boult Je Boult Thiboult or Thibault, or probably De-Bolt — There are many families of the name of Thibault in Flanders Briton Poitiers Berry Dauphine & and of Thiboult in Isle de France Normandy & and there is reason to believe that Some of them were driven from France at the Revocation of the Edict of Nantes, and that they settled in the South and west of England as clever and Industrious people —

There is a tradition in the Jeboult family that they came into this Country at that time, So that as no account of the Jeboults Can

'Particulars' of Edward Jeboult's family.

100

ABOVE LEFT: William James Jeboult, son of James and Harriet, born 1822; CENTRE: their daughter, Caroline, died 1911; RIGHT: their fourth son George, who died young in Torquay; BELOW LEFT: John Barter, who married CENTRE: James Jeboult's daughter Ellen; RIGHT; Louisa Jane (née Brown) who married James' son, Henry Pounsbery Jeboult, and died in 1865, aged 33.

Mr Edward Jeboult
Has been known to me
some years. He is a
man of very high character
in every way, & superior
in intelligence & varied
information
Haygrass &c?
19 June 08

Turnpike Trust Offices, Taunton.
February 4th 1869

In April 1868, the Surveyor of the above
Trust having left suddenly, the Trustees
appointed Mr Edward Jeboult to the office
pro-tem.

At the election in July last, there
were 22 applicants — Mr Easton obtained
21 votes: Mr Jeboult 17. Mr Dangar 1, no
other candidate got a vote

The Trustees expressed their satisfaction
in the way Mr Jeboult had discharged
his duties during his time of office, by
voting him nearly double the amount
of Salary agreed upon. —

W. Upham

(Clerk to the said Trustees)

ABOVE: Edward's son Frank 'was generally very popular — especially amongst ladies'; he married the widow of his New South Wales employer, Mr Miller; here she holds the swing rope in a family group; LEFT: Edward Jeboult secures a reference to his 'very high character', and RIGHT: is rewarded with 'exactly double . . . the salary' as temporary surveyor to the Turnpike Trust in 1869.

The History of West Somerset,

Including a general description of this most interesting District; its Formation, Geology, Soil, &c.; the Customs, Habits and Dialect of its Inhabitants at various times; particulars of the Arts, Manufactures and Agricultural Pursuits; description of its Hills, Moors, Abbeys, Castles, Camps, Roads, Rivers, Canals, Railways, &c., with numerous interesting Extracts from the Books and Papers of many talented Authors, and from the published and unpublished Papers of the Somersetshire Archæological Society, &c., &c.

Dedicated (by permission) to F. M. BISSET, Esq., High Sheriff of the County.

A DETAILED ACCOUNT OF

The Valley of the Tone,

Including a description of this beautiful Neighbourhood and of each of its Sixty Parishes, its Towns, Churches, Schools, Charities, Area, Population, Manufactures, Soil, Situation; its Owners, Principal Inhabitants, &c.; Ancient History and Customs, useful information respecting Post-office, Union, Hundred, Archdeaconry and Parochial subjects.

Dedicated (by desire) to Lord ARTHUR HERVEY, Bishop of the Diocese.

The History of the Town of Taunton,

From its rise to the present time, including the Castle, Churches, Chapels, Public Offices, Buildings and Companies, Colleges, Schools, Charities, &c., &c.; also Parliamentary, Local and other Information, Epitome of Principal Events, List of Eminent Men, Duties of the Town Officers, Names of Local Authors, the Mansions in the Neighbourhood, Villages and their Distances, and an account of Election of Members of Parliament down to the present time, &c., &c.

This History has been nearly ten years in hand, and was prepared under the express patronage of the late Lord TAUNTON.

By EDWARD JEBOULT (Amator Patriæ),

SURVEYOR, &c., 23, HIGH-STREET, TAUNTON.

It is nearly 80 years since any history of this part of the County was issued, and more than 50 years since the last history of Taunton appeared, and no expense or trouble has been spared in the present work, which is embraced in nearly 400 large pages demy quarto (12 inches by 9). Excellent type, on beautiful toned paper, handsomely bound, and profusely illustrated with 136 views of the principal Churches, Gentlemen's Seats, Castles, Abbeys and other Public Buildings throughout this portion of the County, and a Map of the Neighbourhood.

The Views are executed by the new process of

HELIOTYPE,

Being its introduction into this neighbourhood. They are taken from photographs, printed with ink, and not liable to be effaced by time.

Among the 136 Heliotypic Views will be found the following :—

CHURCHES.—Taunton St. Mary's, St. James', St. John's, Wilton, Bridgwater (3), Wellington, Ilminster, Chard, Dunster, Martock, North Curry, Staple Fitzpaine, Durston, Bradford, Nynehead, Crowcombe, Halse, Bishop's Lydeard, Ash Priors, Staplegrove, Norton, Fitzhead, Buckland St. Mary, Huish, Brent, Corfe, Bishop's Hull, West Hatch, Angersleigh, Bagborough, Kingston, Trull, Cheddon, West Buckland, Pitminster, Creech, Lyng, Stoke, Thorn, Hatch, Curry Mallet, Heathfield, &c., &c.

GENERAL VIEWS of Taunton, Bridgwater, Dunster, Williton, Wellington, Ilminster, Wiveliscombe, Watchet, Minehead, Bishop's Lydeard, Stoke, Corfe.

Amongst the SEATS OF THE NEIGHBOURING GENTRY will be found—Montacute, Orchard Wyndham, Sandhill, Walford, Lyngford, Crowcombe Court, Bagborough House, Halswell, Hestercombe, St. Audries, Nettlecombe, Norton Manor, Belmont, Quantock Lodge, Cricket St. Thomas, Heatherton Park, Bishop's Hull Manor House, Netherclay, Culmhead, Batt's Park, Orchard Portman, Grove House, Pinkhurst, The Elms, Breadlands, and many others.

The RECTORIES of St. Mary's, Taunton, Staplegrove, Buckland St. Mary, Bagborough, West Monkton, Trull, Staple Fitzpaine, Stoke St. Gregory, Lympsham, Angersleigh, &c., &c.

COLLEGES AND SCHOOLS.—The Old and New Taunton Colleges, the Wesleyan and Independents' ditto, Batt's, Fullands, Corfe, Hope House, &c., &c.

CASTLES AND ABBEYS of Taunton, Bridgwater, Dunster, Enmore, Old Cleeve, Muchelney.

PUBLIC BUILDINGS, &c.—Wellington Monument, Taunton Hospital, Bridgwater Old Market Cross, Gates and Bridge, Taunton Convent, numerous Street Views, &c., &c.

Among the 48 additional Photographs will be found the following MANSIONS :—Montacute, Brimpton, Monty's Court, Brymore, Bishop's Hull Manor House, Norton Manor, Halsway, Stoke, Monkton House, Woodlands, Enmore, &c., &c.

Eight Views of Cleeve and Muchelney ABBEYS.

The Churches of St. Mary's, St. John's and St. George's (Taunton), Wiveliscombe, Langport, Kingsbury, Ruishton, Stoke, &c., &c.

PRICES:

In cloth binding, without views	15s.
About 400 large pages, well bound, with 130 illustrations and map	20s.
Ditto, handsomely bound, gilt covers, red edges	25s.
Ditto, ditto, with gilt edges and 48 photographs in addition to the 130 heliotypes	30s.

Copies have been ordered by the High Sheriff of the County, the Bishop of the Diocese, the Members of the County and Borough, the Lord of the Manor, the Rural Dean, and many other gentlemen of influence.

ATTENTION IS PARTICULARLY DIRECTED TO THE ANNEXED TESTIMONIALS.

P. T. O.

The prospectus for Edward Jeboult's published work, *The History of West Somerset,* published in 1873.

Some annecdotes stories & legends connected [with] the JEBOULT family [to] those whom descended — Jocular tradition said "The Jebusites" but on reading what a bad lot they it was decided that it must have been by some more respectable ancestors — and that the idea should be that we came over from Brittany in France at the revocation of the Edict of Nantes

Unfortunately we can find no Jeboults in France or the Channel Islands, So probably the [...] was changed, or all cleared out

My father used to tell a queer story of the death of a little Tommy Jeboult aged about 2 or 3 years who was duly coffined & [laid] in an upper room — His brother Jimmy aged 4 years missed him as a play fellow & after being put to bed commenced a search for Tommy — The coffin was on a chair up there Jimmy climbed but his weight tipped up all the lot and Poor Tommy was uncoffined & lay on the floor of the room The Parents below rushed up, but Jimmy was found in bed frightened but quiet & denied all knowledge of Thomas. until some weeks after Jimmy in his sleep was heard to say "Tommy come out & Jimmy run" or bolted perhaps he said "I bolt" which as J & I are alike may have given rise to the strange name —

When Jimmy was about 12 years old he was sent to Wilton orchard with his uncle, this was opposite the churchyard in which he [saw] a "ghost" "[with] waving arms all dressed in white As the creature raised its arms Jimmy saw a pair of Red Stockings on the legs & as only his uncles man servant sported so showy a color Jimmy identified the ghost So he laid the horse whip across the red legs when a voice exclaimed Oh don't e Ma[ster] Jimmie tis only I & no ghost —

'Some anecdotes stories and legends connected with the JEBOULT family' in Edward Jeboult's hand.

Edward Jeboult — in his final illness, 1893. His wife sits on the left; to the right stand his daughters Rosie and Florence. The faithful family dog guards his master as he works on the pages of the second edition of his published book, reprinted posthumously. The illustrated story of his town had to wait another 90 years for publication as *Jeboult's Taunton.*

BIBLIOGRAPHY

The factual basis for this study, apart from Jeboult's own manuscript volumes, has been principally local newspapers. Files used include those of the *Western Flying Post* or *Sherborne Mercury, Taunton Courier, Somerset County Gazette* and *Somerset County Herald*. Additional information has been drawn from the parish records (particularly vestry minutes and rate books) of St Mary's, St James's and Wilton, and the minutes of the Turnpike Trust, Market Trust, Local Board of Health and Corporation. All these, together with the newspaper files, are deposited at the Somerset Record Office. Details of the 19th century Taunton College School were obtained from the scrapbooks of Rev William Tuckwell, held by King's College. A list of local and national directories used will be found in my *Book of Taunton* (1977), p. 143.

Alford, H., *Taunton Health Reports* (1873-8)
Askwith, W.H., *The Church of St Mary Magdalene, Taunton* (1908)
Cottle, J., *Brief Memoir . . . of a Young Disciple of Jesus* (1839)
Cottle, J., *Church of St Mary Magdalene, Taunton* (1845)
Goldsworthy, E.F., *Reminiscences of Taunton* (4th edn. 1975)
Jeboult, E., *History of West Somerset* (1873, 1893)
Kite, G.H., and H.P. Palmer, *Taunton, its History and Market Trust* (1926)
Page, W. (ed.), *Victoria History of Somerset,* ii (1911)
Peake, T.H. (ed.), *Taunton Workhouse, 1847-9* (Taunton School, n.d.)
Somerset & Dorset Notes & Queries
Taunton of Today (1895)
Thomas, D. St J., *Regional History of the Railways of Great Britain* (1960)
Webb, C.G., *History of Taunton* (1874)

Numbers in *italics* refer to illustrations

111

SUBSCRIBERS

Presentation Copies

1 Taunton Deane Borough Council
2 Somerset County Council
3 Taunton Public Library
4 Somerset Local History Library
5 Somerset Record Office
6 Somerset County Museum
7 Somerset Archaeological & Natural History Society
8 Mrs Constance Gray Read

9 Robin Bush
10 Clive & Carolyn Birch
11 Peter Birch
12 Alexander Bush
13 Catherine Bush
14 John Summerhayes Jeboult
15 Constance Gray Read
16 Merryn Gray Smith
17 Tamsin Creyghton Smith
18 Jodie Anne Smith
19 Zenophy Jane Smith
20 Alexander Gray Smith
21 Glynn Gray Read
22 Oliver Gray Read
23 Julian Gray Read
24 Mercy D. Palmer
25 R.E. Webb
26
28 Mr & Mrs A. Tilly
29 Hilary Marshall
30 A.A. Johnston
31 Rev & Mrs G.C.H. Watson
32 A.G. Ellard
33 Mrs J.M. Braund
34 John C.B. Hunt
35 E.S. North
36 Peter Chard
37 James F. Coker
38 W.R. Hadley
39 Victoria & Albert Museum
40 Mr & Mrs Allsworth
41 Lornie Leete-Hodge
42 F.J. Burridge
43 Mrs M.J. Walker
44 D.F. Eckless
45 Mr & Mrs J.I. Punter
46 Geoff Thomas & Son
47 Field Studies Council, Taunton
48 Michael T. Day
49 E.J. Harris
50 Andrew White
51 John & Shirley Driver
52 Major & Mrs R. Clooney
53 Michael Bird
54 Rosemary A. Sixsmith
55 Mrs Christine Brown

56 L.A. Haldane
57 Rt Hon Edward Du Cann MP
58 Dr A.H.T. Robb-Smith
59 D.W. Joyce
60 Malcolm R. Upham
61 Miss N.J. Taylor
62 Priorswood Primary School
63 John Frederick Dowell
64 R.I. Churchill
65 Reg & Lesley Arberry
66 Ian Matthews
67 Peter & Bridget Lyall
68 Mrs L.J. Price
69 Janice Marfell
70 Colin Turner
71 Barrie Pitt
72
73 Michael Robinson
74 Mrs Kathleen Willett
75 L.J. McHardy
76 Mr & Mrs K.J. Miller
77 Mrs B.A. Parsons
78 Miss Annette Brenan
79 Kenneth Baker
80 T.W. Mayberry
81 Mrs J. Walsh
82 Margaret Larkworthy
83 F.R. Jarvis
84 Paula Lewis
85 Mrs E.M. Calver
86 Mrs V. Northey
87 Mrs J. Woodford
88 Mrs A. Farrant
89 Penny Stanbury
90 Dr John Speller
91 T.L. Tutcher
92 Pat Wolseley
93 Mrs P. Broach
94 M.D. Hollands
95 Mrs R. Elliott
96 Tim & Joy Robinson
97 Jane & Peter Hotchkis
98 Fred Clarke
99 E.W. Spiller
100 Mrs G. Foster
101 Mrs Yvonne Browning
102 Christine Warren

103 Harold J. Potter
104 J.F. Glanfield
105 F.W. A'Court
106 Mrs M. Staple
107 M. Hawkes
108 Dorothy N.M. Bakeley
109 Prudence D.M. Coad
110 L.H. Cornish
111 A.F.P. Richards
112 Claire Griffin
113 Gordon Thorne
114 Miss Pamela Thorne
115 Lyndon Herbert Dyer
116 D.J. Gill
117 Guy Tidmarsh
118 Margot Burgess
119 Mrs P. Foster
120 Mrs Margaret McCowat
121 Mrs C. Robinson
122 Mrs S.A. Beney
123 G.G. Webb
124 K.T. Glanville
125 A.S. Turner
126 Mrs M. Burgess
127 Mr & Mrs D.T. Stutt
128 Mrs N. Gerrard
129 Mrs M. Sutton
130 Mrs P.J. Millwood
131 Mrs S. Jordan
132 Mr & Mrs R.A. Bayliss
133 Mr & Mrs P.A. Davey
134 Mrs G.O. Murphy
135 Mrs Sheila Longman
136 Miss M. Sherren
137 Miss Joan D. Peden
138 Peter Anthony Moore
139 Mrs G.F. Small
140 W. Dudley Hunt
141 Ewart Dawes BEM
142 Mrs D. Knighton
143 Richard Harrison
144 W.J. Parratt
145 David Hall
146 Brian Stuckey
147 R. Evis
148 Mrs Jean Jackson

149	L.T. Caddy	215	M.A. Gibbs	280	Mrs I. Gould
150	J. Snooks	216	W.T.C. Stephens	281	John Pugh
151	Mrs B.L. Gamblin	217	Miss P. Challenger	282	Frank A. Smith
152	Mrs Florence S. Woodman	218	James Victor Winter	283	M.E. Quick
153	Mrs Anne Parsons	219	S. Wild	284	Mrs Rosa Simpson-Jagers
154	H&E Chapman	220	Mrs Margaret Riley	285	Kenneth Arthur Horne
155	Richard Viant	221	Rachel & David Willcox	286	John Anthony Terry
156	Malcolm Hedge	222	Roger & Shirley Mason	287	Rosemary & Roy Hayman
157	J.M. Melville	223	David & Brenda Janes	288	Ian & Janet Paynter
158	M.J. Taylor	224	Christopher & Jan Rimmer	289	Jeanne & Julian Smith
159	T. Golesworthy	225	Dennis Morrell	290	Eileen Thorpe
160	Mrs E. Salter	226	Mrs C.A. Crouch	291	John, Shirley & Paul Croker
161	Mrs Lola H. Anderton	227	F.G. Randle	292	Libby Webber
162	H.W. Bond	228	Leonard Oaten	293	Peter & Jennifer Smith
163	Stella Wilson	229	Nigel Daniell	294	Gordon & Grace Macdonald
164	B.M. Buddridge	230	Antony & Audrey Middleton	295	David Lea
165	Frances & Don Walker	231	J.C. Napper	296	Roger Lea
166	Mr & Mrs R.W.J. Cole	232	Reg Long	297	Mrs Joy Sparrow
167	A.G. Constable	233	John Schroder	298	Jean Kelly
168	J.M. Close	234	Mr & Mrs E.C. Parsons	299	Ronald Garbett
169	D.A. & M.W. Shepherd	235	J. Rennie	300	A.A. Webber
170	T.H. Peake	236	E.F. Binning	301	Bryan & Susan McEnroe
171	I.J. Newbold	237	Miss G.M. Farmer	302	W.J. Marshall
172	R.C. Dunning	238	I. Higson	303	R.E. Willcox
173 174	J.T. Bennett	239	Susan F. Merrell	304	R.D.P. Haines
175 176	Ewart Dawes BEM	240	Major E.H. Vaulter	305	J.E.B. Kite
		241	Mrs A. Jeffery	306	E.J. Harris
177	Mrs A.R. Colledge	242	Derek Arthur Smith	307	R.A. Field
178	Brian Derrick	243	Lynn Wells	308	Mrs B.G. Drake-Brockman
179 181	Mr & Mrs A. Tilly	244	S.D. Berry	309	Charles & Betty Lane
		245	Jose Hrydziuszko	310	Mrs Sylvia McLeod
182	Mrs Diana Ruffell	246	Major E.S. Briant	311	Mrs M.A. Titterton
183	Gerald Hartland	247	Mrs J.M. Broom	312	Clement J. Broomfield
184	Jack Chapman	248	A. Derrick	313	Felicity Matthews
185	A.H. Vernon	249	Mr & Mrs S. Marsh	314	Maurice Leakey
186	Mrs Shirley G. Pielou	250 251	Mercy D. Palmer	315	Iris & Geoffrey Preston
187	Isla Rowlands			316	Mrs M.B. Sanders
188	Mrs Betty Footitt	252	R.E. Webb	317	Mrs B. Rees
189	Morris Williams ARIBA AILA	253	F.J. A'Court	318 321	M.W. & H. Street
190	Brian J. Heaton	254	Nigel Langdon		
191	Terry Ravenor ARCM	255	W.R. Langdon	322	Mr & Mrs Neil B. Trood
192	Miss Phyllis M. Male	256	Daniel James Talbot	323	Mr & Mrs Roger Manning
193	Donald W.D. Pearce	257	Mrs A.M. Goble	324	G.C. Tarr
194	E.M. McLennan	258	E.G. Elliott	325	Mrs D.A. Norton
195	Miss Valerie A. Couch	259	Eric C. Lawrance	326	J.M. Moore
196	J. Parrott	260	Dorothy Shearman	327	Miss Hazell Organ
197	E.A. Perry	261	Brent Disney-Walford	328	Audrey & Gordon Holcombe
198	Peter Yates	262	G.M. Denham	329	Linda Symonds
199	A.P. Berry	263	G.M.S. Belshaw	330	Vincenzo Pizii
200	Wg Cdr & Mrs L. Hague	264	Joy E. Darby	331	Beehive School
201	Jonathan I. Hague	265	Mrs A.L. Callen	332	Duncan Furner
202	A.T. Colbeck	266	R.M. Walker	333 334	Derek T. Cole
203	Dorothy Burnett	267	Mrs Lorna C. Johnston		
204	Miss Vera Cooper	268	H.R. Gready	335	Mrs Pat Sharman
205	H.F. Burnett	269	Mrs A.E. Appleton	336	Pauline E. Goldsworthy
206	T.G. Hiscock	270	Mrs Dorothy J. Bond	337	John & Linda Cole
207	R.F. Winckworth	271 272	C.E. Bond	338	Elizabeth Naylor
208	Mr & Mrs G.A. Gunn			339	Mr & Mrs John Naylor
209	R.G. Coles	273	Mrs R.G.P. Besley	340	Sue Berry
210	Carol A. Sydenham	274	Betty I. Cowdy	341	Mr & Mrs F. Berry
211	Mr & Mrs W.G. Perry	275	Mrs B. Shepherd	342	Prudence D.M. Coad
212	D.M. Hartnell	276	Rev K. Wilkinson Riddle	343	Mrs S. Everett
213	Mrs Sylvia Barsby	277	W. Berry	344	Miss Helen M. Russell
214	Marian Gould	278	Paul Rye	345	P.J. Gange
		279	Rachel E. Anderdon	346	Miss I.M. Ash

347	Michael & Maureen Rowland	412	Dr P. Hickman	475	W.F.A. Sellick
348	Mr & Mrs K.E. Handoll	413	G.E.A. Lane	476	Eamonn Platt
349	Nicholas Molland	414	Mrs R.E. Bodey	477	Mrs M.J. Chetwynd
350	Richard Dinwiddy	415	L.R. Beck	478	D.F. Kodritsch
351	Mrs P.H. Huggill	416	Arthur Bending ARCM ARCO	479	Mrs J. Ollgrove
352	M.W. Passmore		LTCL	480	J. Bament
353	Mrs M.M. Martin	417	Mrs R. Besley	481	St Augustine of Canterbury's
354	E. Nash	418	E.W. Mead	482	School
355	Pauline Moon	419	L.G. Coleman	483	
356	David P. Salter	420	P. Porter	485	Ladymead School
357	Valerie & Michael Hine	421	Alistair Wolseley	486	B.R. Cleaver
358	L.A. Fivash	422	Heather Wolseley	487	Ms Lindsay Choffin
359	Mrs Helen Dolley	423	T.N. Snow	488	R. Batten
360	M. Tratt	424	K.H. Rogers	489	Mr & Mrs D. Manuel
361	Mrs G.M. Collis	425	C.P. Collard	490	A. Stocker
362	Louis Forsyth	426	Adrian & Gill Whatmore	491	Mrs A. Parish
363	Miss Julie Deacon	427	Philip & Sally Twiss	492	Charles Winter
364	Edwina M. Swain	428	Miss Susan Rigg	493	A.J. Hearn
365	J.M. & C.J. Cutting	429	G. Caddy	494	Dr & Mrs A.H. Bakker
366	Ivor & Pat Dew	430	B.J. Goodhall	495	David Greenfield
367	K.J. Hocking	431	Tom & Jackie Murrow	496	Mike White
368	Miss Freda Dawe BEM	432	A.C. Spurling	497	Margaret Bond
369	David Malcolm Doig	433	Mrs M.C. Henson	498	Philip Lewis
370	R.H. Swan	434	R.M. Dugdale	499	S.D. Hobbs
		435	Francis Darlow	500	David C. Lawrence
371	S.K. Gooding	436		501	Jeffrey R. Rogers
372	Chris Dew	437	R.R. Snook	502	W.E. Perry
373	Michael & Marlene Slocombe	438	Eric H. Hall	503	Mr & Mrs R.S. Crane
374	David Gledhill	439	Mr & Mrs R.W. Holt	504	Mrs Doris Walker
375	J.A. Reeves	440	L.W. Hawkins	505	John Reynolds
376	D.L. Craufurd	441	Mr & Mrs R. Deane	506	Mr & Mrs R.J. Salter
377	Miss J.M. Sully	442	J. Patch	507	A.D. Hayward
378	Dr St C.M. L'A Hubbard	443	R.A. Salde OBE	508	C.F. Clements
379	Marion Cameron	444	Brian & Linda Singh	509	Michael & Jean Hole
380	Andrew Harewood	445	A.A. Gamble	510	N.R. Chipchase
381	Miss F.K. Cornish	446	Mrs E. Habberfield	511	Captain N.E. Upham
382	Mrs H.C. List	447	Ronald Sams	512	James Skeggs
383	Linda & Michael Skinner	448	Gordon Bird	513	Randall Davis
384	Kate Rhianydd Porter	449	W.J. Gardner	514	G.A. Jordan
385	Col C.T. Mitford Slade	450	Miss J. Pitman	515	Brian J. Murless
386	Jeremy John Leyton	451	L. Snow	516	Mrs Helena M. Dodge
387	G. Homer	452	A.W. Frost	517	J.W.J. Dodman
388	Mr & Mrs L.J. Keating	453	M.C. Fishlock	518	Mrs S.H. Billinge
389	Mrs J. Parrish	454	J. Thomas	519	Michael C.J. Darch
390	Geoff & Kath Lawford	455	S. Boon	520	M.R. Upham
391	Marion Harding	456	Mrs Delia Spiller	521	Miss B.M. Harris
392	Richard & Elinor Samuel	457	Harold & Joyce Binding	522	R.J. Burrough
393	Mr & Mrs J.C. Laver	458	Dr K.W.T. Caddy	523	Mrs M. Miles
394	G.W. & P.M. Gale	459	Mr & Mrs H. Holt	524	Mrs O.K. Thrift
395	R.J. Puchoras	460	R.W. Beale	525	G.C. Merrifield
396	F.K. Kenne MBE	461	E.A. Park	526	D.G. Richards
397	Mr & Mrs D. Rimmer	462	C.M. Bagehot Kite	527	John B. Bentley
398	F.J. Hutchin	463	George W. Hill	528	Roger Alan Hagley
399	Cherry Hitchcock	464	Sefton Anthony Edward Charles	529	Mr & Mrs Berry
400	Mrs J. Giscocks		Disney	530	A.G. Williams
401	R.J. Dight	465	Mrs M.E. Matthewson	531	Ronald E.H. Hayman
402	J.A.R. Cheal	466	J.F. Howell	532	Reg Moggridge
403	Miss H. Barry Long	467	Rev Alan Beck AKC	533	R.G. Fogwill
404	L.E. Johnson	468	Alex & Mary Yandall	534	Miss P.J. Tytherleigh
405	Tony & Janet Fowler	469	T.H. Peake	535	V.J. Wrigley
406	Mrs A. Bishop	470	K.R. Lang	536	R.C.H. Pendleton
407	Claire Botcherby	471	Madeline M.A. Roberts	537	Katherine & Ross Ward
408	Stephen Botcherby	472	Mable Owen	538	Madeline M.A. Roberts
409	A.G. Ellard	473	Roger & Lynne Nash	539	Mable Owen
410	Mrs Hazel M. Bowers	474	Robin J. Turney	540	H. Evison
411	Mrs Doris Trott				

541 K.J. & E.J. Miller	570 B.G. & P.M. Vine	599 Leonard Arthur Cross
542 Mrs Nicky Matthews	571 B.J. Nutbeem	600 Mrs Jean Colquhoun
543 Barbara Viant	572 N.E. Whiting	601 Martin J. Howe
544 W. Hollinrake CBE	573 W.J. Cross	602 Nicola Howe
545 E.G. Webb	574 Mrs V.W. von Tyszka	603 H.H. Withers
546 K.T. Glanville	575 Mrs E.E. Robinson	604 Frederick George Dowell
547 P.E.F. Chetwynd	576 Mr & Mrs G. Manuel	605 A.E. Oaten
548 G.W.W. Markwick	577 J.L. Randle	606 Keith Boobyer
549 Dr H.D. Fleming	578 Miss Lynne A. Willoughby	607 L.F. Daymond Johns
550 J.F. Williams	579 D.H. Burns	608 David Griffin
551 Mr & Mrs R.F. Troup	580 A.C. Crossing	609 Rev R.F. Acworth
552 C.M. Bagehot Kite	581 Mrs P.A. Ranson	610 Miss M.J. Harvey
553 Ronald & Claudine Tickner	582 R.W. Bond	611 Mrs M.J. Palmer
554 J. Sully	583 N.S. D'Cruz	612 Mr & Mrs Allsworth
555 David J. Sparks	584 W. Pinn	613 Lee Griffin
556 Mr & Mrs G.M. Adams	585 D. Perry	614 Ms C.H. Jarvis
557 Mr & Mrs N.H. Law	586 Mrs C.R. Selwood	615 Kenneth Baker
558 M.G. Hunter	587 Mrs J. Weaver	616 Fred Clarke
559 Mrs J.E.A. Whitehead	588 Mrs Jean Carrow	617 Charles Bray
560 Donald L. Crewe	589 F.G. Hartnell	618
561 P.J. & B.E. Lippiatt	590 Mrs Lorna Saunders	642 Somerset County Library
562 R. Northam	591 Mr & Mrs R.F. Benham	643 Mrs Margaret Sumption
563 Edwin Parker	592 John A. Hamlin	644 Mrs M.L. Hunt
564 Mr & Mrs E.G. Pike	593 Mrs I.P.D. Skinner	645 Marion & Michael Harrison
565 Stuart & Christine Trott	594 Mr & Mrs E.C. Hillman	646 Mrs Noreen Selway
566 V. Yuill	595 Mrs Valerie Fitzpatrick	647 Albert Pepper
567 J.M. Rosewell	596 Mrs Joan W. Trott	648 Somerset and Dorset Family
568 I.A. Jenkins	597 Mr & Mrs W. Morris	653 History Society
569 Nick Warboys	598 Don & Margaret Archer	654 Miss Lily Willies
		655 A.D. Wood
		656 Kevin & Rowena Smith

Remaining names unlisted.

ENDPAPERS — FRONT: Wood's map of Taunton 1840; BACK:
Taunton 1885.